Presents

Rusty Cooley's
Arpeggio Madness
Insane Concepts & Total Mastery

Method By Rusty Cooley

Supervising Editor: John McCarthy
Music Transcribing & Engraving: Jimmy Rutkowski
Production Manager: John McCarthy
Layout, Graphics & Design: Jimmy Rutkowski

Copy Editor: Cathy McCarthy

Cover Art Direction & Design:
Jimmy Rutkowski

HL173375
ISBN: 978-1-4950-6948-2
Produced by John McCarthy®
© 2016 McCarthy Publishing, LLC All Rights Reserved

Table of Contents

Digital eBook 3
Icon Key.. 4
Rusty's Words of Wisdom 6
Tuning... 7
Sweep Picking Technique..................... 8

Chapter 1:
A Minor Five &
Six String Root Shapes 10
Chapter 2:
C Major Five & Six
String Arpeggio Shapes...................... 15
Chapter 3:
B Diminished Arpeggios 19
Chapter 4:
Three to Five String
Arpeggio Sequences 22
Chapter 5:
Melodic Arpeggios 25
Chapter 6:
Fifth String Root Sevenths.................. 28
Chapter 7:
Additional Seventh
Arpeggio Concepts.............................. 36
Chapter 8:
Combining Arpeggios with
Chromatic Passing Tones................... 38

Program 2

Chapter 9:
Diatonic 11th Arpeggios in the
Key of "G" Major 39
Chapter 10:
Diatonic 13th Arpeggios in the
Key of "G" Major 42
Chapter 11:
Extended Diatonic Arpeggios in the
Key of "G" Major 44
Chapter 12:
Diatonic 13th Arpeggios in the
Key of "B" Harmonic Minor 47
Chapter 13:
Four String 5ths Arpeggios................. 51
Chapter 14:
Sweeping 5ths Key of "C" Major......... 53
Chapter 15:
Two String Seep Picking
Arpeggio Sequence............................. 54
Chapter 16:
Two-String Economy Picking
Arpeggio Sequence............................. 58
Chapter 17:
Diminished 7th Arpeggios
Sweep Picking...................................... 59
Chapter 18:
Applying Diminished 7th Arpeggios
Using Legato 61
Chapter 19:
Three Octave String Skipping
Legato Arpeggios................................. 63
Chapter 20:
Three Octave Arpeggios
with Tapping... 65
Chapter 21:
String Skipping Legato Solo 67

BONUS LESSONS
Chapter 22:
Single String Triads "Death Licks" 69
Chapter 23:
Song Excerpts from Rusty.................. 73
"Diminium" 73
"Riders".. 74
"Riders" - Chorus Arpeggios &
Outro Solo 75
"The Butcher" - Intro 76
"The Butcher" - Pre Solo..................... 77
"War Cry" 78

Chord Table 79

Digital eBook & Video

When you register this product at the lesson support site RockHouseMethod.com, you will receive a digital version of this book. This interactive eBook can be used on all devices that support Adobe PDF. This will allow you to access your book using the latest portable technology any time you want. You will also recieve access to video tutorials that correspond with the lessons in this book.

Use this member number to register for Lesson Support at RockHouseMethod.com

AM993785

Icon Key

These tell you there is additional information and learning utilities available at RockHouseSchool.com to support that lesson.

Backing Track

Backing track icons are placed on lessons where there is an audio demonstration to let you hear what that lesson should sound like or a backing track to play the lesson over. Use these audio tracks to guide you through the lessons. **Use your member number to register at the** *Lesson Support* **site and download the corresponding audio tracks.**

Metronome

Metronome icons are placed next to the examples that we recommend you practice using a metronome. You can download a free, adjustable metronome on the *Lesson Support* site.

Worksheet

Worksheets are a great tool to help you thoroughly learn and understand music. These worksheets can be downloaded at the *Lesson Support* site.

Tuner

You can download the free online tuner on the *Lesson Support* site to help tune your instrument.

About the Instructor

Rusty Cooley

Rusty Cooley is at the forefront of pushing the boundaries of modern guitar playing. A world renown musician and instructor who has influenced some of today's most respected guitarist such as Mark Tremonti of Creed and John Petrucci of Dreamtheater – he has performed on more than 15 albums and has seven different instructional products to his credit. His two new products Fretboard Autopsy Level 1 and Fretboard Autopsy Level 2 from Rock House have been his most well received and critically acclaimed instructional products to date.

Rusty has been featured in magazines such as Guitar Player, Guitar One, Guitar World, Guitar Techniques and Axe. He has had his own column in Guitar Player magazine titled "Metal Guru." In January 2003, Rusty was given the honor of the "7th Fastest Shredder of All Time" by Guitar One Magazine and most recently was named by Total Guitar magazine as one of the top 20 fastest shredders of all time.

Rusty has his own signature model guitar with Dean, the "RC7 Xenocide" released in 2007, He uses EMG pickups, Diamond Amplification, Morley, Intellitouch tuners, Rocktron preamps, Maxon, GHS strings, VHT, Conklin and Eventide harmonizers.

For more information on Rusty and his instructional products visit RockHouseMethod.com.

Rusty's Words of Wisdom

Arpeggios are usually considered a pretty advanced subject, and often times found to be difficult by players that don't understand how they are derived musically or even how they work. By definition, arpeggio simply means the notes of a chord played separately. A strong foundation in visualizing your neck will go a long way to fully gaining the most from this program as well as getting the most mileage from your arpeggio usage. If you do not have a strong ability to visualize your neck, it is suggested that you work through the Rock House Fretboard Autopsy programs first. These programs will help you to see all of the notes within your keys as well as all of the arpeggio possibilities that are available to you. Being able to visualize your entire Fretboard will allow you to blend your chords, scales and arpeggios together as you melodically burn up and down the neck of your guitar easily and with the freedom you are looking for as a great guitarist.

Tuning

For all of the examples in this program Rusty has his guitar tuned down a half step to Eb. Also, Rusty is using a seven-string guitar, so pay close attention to the examples on the corresponding video. If you are not used to playing a seven-string guitar, you may be disoriented as to which string he is on. A seven string guitar has a low B string above the low E string on a standard six-string guitar. However, keep in mind that you don't need a seven-string guitar to follow along with the lessons in this program.

The easiest and most accurate way to tune your guitar is to use an electronic tuner. There are different kinds available that are fairly inexpensive. You can also download the free online tuner from the *Lesson Support site* at RockHouseMethod.com. Here are the tuning notes for this program:

(Thinnest)						(Thickest)
1st String	2nd String	3rd String	4th String	5th String	6th String	7th String
E♭	B♭	G♭	D♭	A♭	E♭	B♭

Note that even though Rusty is using a seven-string guitar, all of the examples he teaches only use the 6th through 1st strings making all of the examples applicable to all guitarists.

For a six-string guitar tune as follows:

(Thinnest)					(Thickest)
1st String	2nd String	3rd String	4th String	5th String	6th String
E♭	B♭	G♭	D♭	A♭	E♭

Sweep Picking Technique

Throughout this program, many of the examples are going to employ the usage of sweep picking. If you are new to this technique, sweep picking is where you use one picking motion to play adjacent strings in a row.

For an ascending sweep, you will use one pick stroke across your strings toward the floor. The key point to remember is that the picking motion regardless of ascending or descending is continuous, you do not pick each string individually, and the motion is similar to downward strumming where the pick just drops lightly across the strings in one smooth movement. When descending, the motion is the same, continuous but in an upward direction.

The second part of the picking hand technique you need to be aware of is string muting. When sweep picking if you do not mute the strings as you play, you will encounter a lot of excessive string noise. To remedy this problem, you will have to use several areas of the palm of your picking hand to mute the strings that are not being played, and, depending on what strings you are playing will determine how much and what parts of your hand you will have to utilize to mute the strings to keep the string noise at a minimum. When sweep picking you will use the areas of your palm that are:

- **Below your pinkie (A)**
- **Below your thumb (B)**
- **The central part just above your wrist (C)**

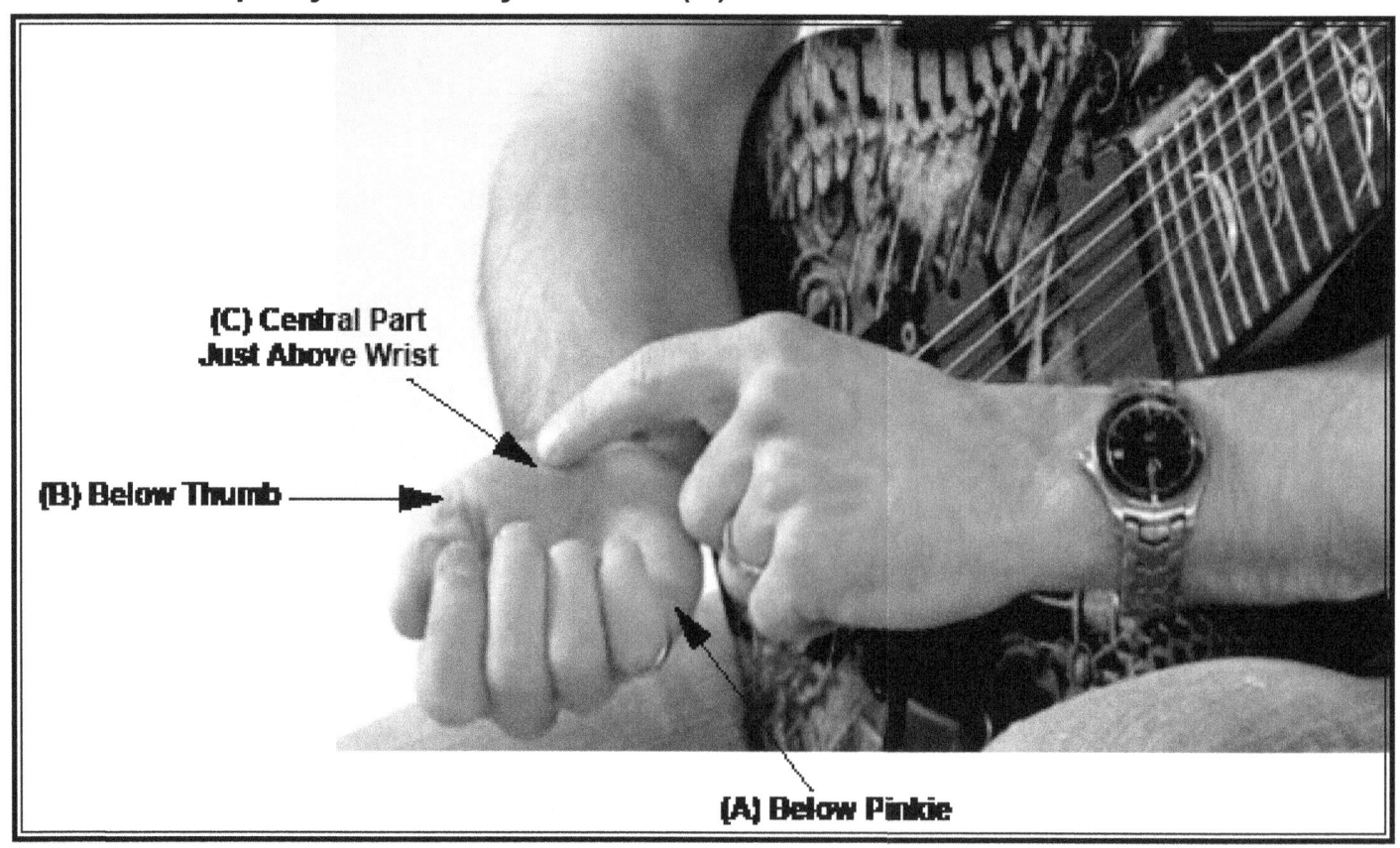

Unlike palm muting when playing rhythm guitar where you primarily use the area of your hand below your pinkie finger (A), you will use these three parts of your hand either individually or all together at the same time.

Lastly, you need to know that the right hand will use a "rolling-bar" technique. For example, if you have an arpeggio where you have to play the 4th string 7th fret and then the 3d string 7th fret with the third finger ascending consecutively, you would play the 4th string with the tip of your third finger, and then roll to the back (or finger pad) of your third finger releasing your finger tip from the 4th string (but still touching it lightly to deaden or mute the 4th string) while simultaneously pressing down the 3 string. If you did not do this and just pressed both strings down together, the notes would ring like a chord, and as stated earlier, an arpeggio by definition is the notes of a chord played "separately." When descending, the finger motion is just the opposite, start on the pad of your finger and roll to the tip of your finger deadening the third string as you roll your finger. You are essentially just reversing the technique.

One last technique, you can also employ a more advanced form of muting and use the outer edge of your first finger to mute the strings. This is a more advanced form of muting, but combined with all of the other key points in this lesson, all excessive string noise should be alleviated and everything should be ringing pretty clearly.

Chapter 1:
A Minor Five & Six String Root Shapes

We are going to begin our journey into arpeggios by learning a series of 5 and 6-string A minor arpeggio shapes. We will begin with three initial shapes that utilize all 6 strings and then two 5-string shapes that are derived from the initial 6-string shapes. The intervallic formula for the minor arpeggio is root - minor third - perfect fifth.

6-String Shape 1

The first arpeggio is going to use all 6 strings. This arpeggio is a root 6th string, 5th fret A minor arpeggio and the picking for this pattern is: Up – Down – Down – Down – Down – Down – Up (pull-off) – Up – Up – Up – Up – Up – Down. This is the same picking pattern you will use for all of the arpeggios in this lesson. Here is your first 6-string shape:

Notes: A - C - E Intervals: 1 ♭3 5

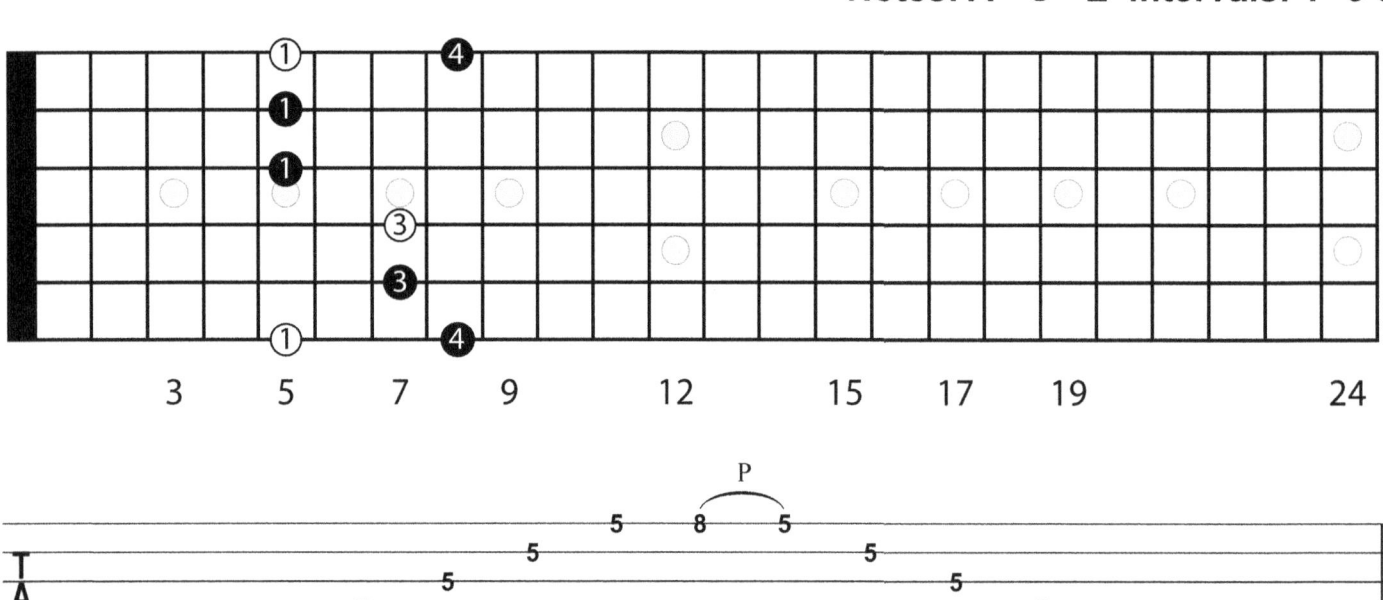

6-String Shape 1 – Derivative 1

The second arpeggio we are going to cover is the first derivative of the 6-string shape 1 arpeggio and it uses strings 2 through 6. In this example, the root note is now played on the 2nd string 10th fret instead of the 1st string 5th fret. Pay close attention to the fingering in this example. The fingering may seem a little foreign and this is due to the stretch on the second string from the 5th fret to the 10th fret. By using the third finger on the 6th string 8th fret, it sets up your pinkie to play the 10th fret on the 2nd string; you will notice that when your third finger is fretting the 8th fret, the pinkie is "hanging-over" the 10th fret. It is important to always finger arpeggios in a way that will allow your hand to easily make the shifts and stretches needed especially when you are sweep picking. The key to effective arpeggio execution is to keep the strings sounding sharp, crisp and clean by maintaining a balance between muting and fingering.

6-String Shape 1 – Derivative 2

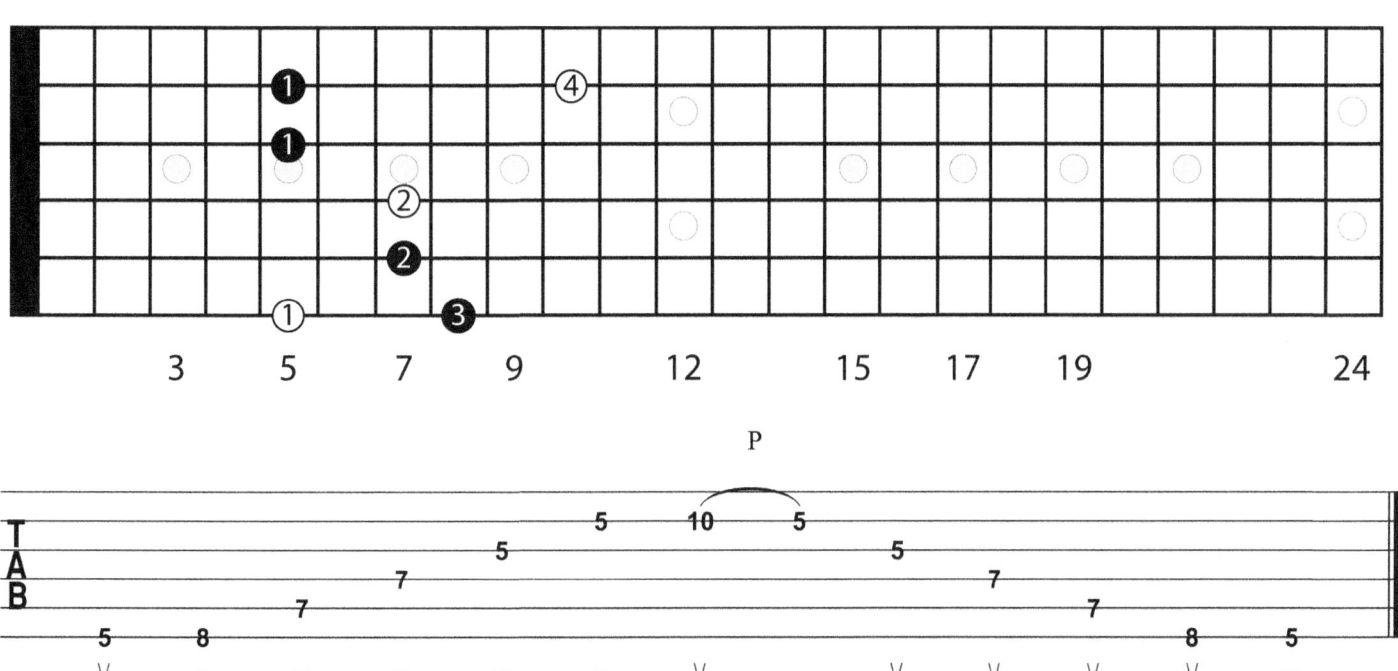

Next up is the 2nd derivative of the first arpeggio shape and uses strings 1 through 5. This arpeggio is a first inversion A minor arpeggio because it begins on the minor third "C." Once again, the fingering is the key to successfully getting the notes to sound clearly. By avoiding a "bar", which would be the most common fingering, you will isolate each fretted note individually. In doing this you will avoid excessive string noise and unwanted ringing notes gaining a cleaner sounding arpeggio.

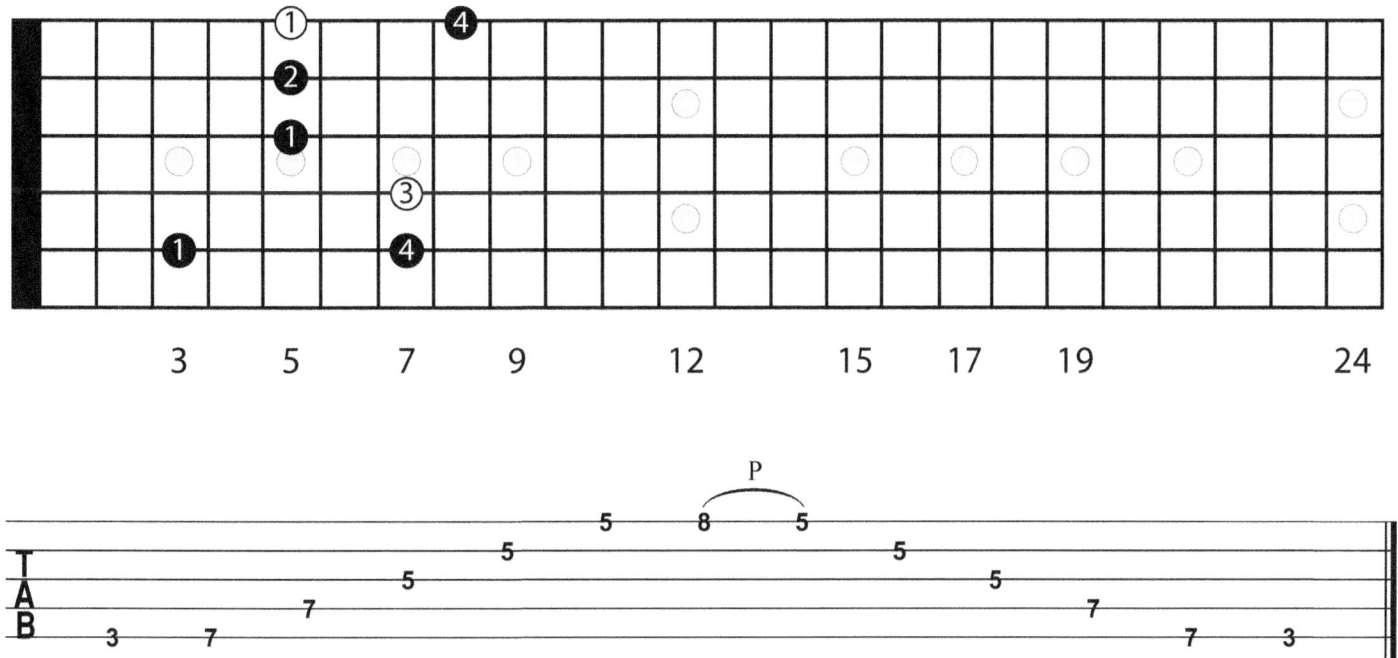

6-String Shape 2

The next arpeggio shape will be a 2 octave A minor shape using all 6 strings and begins on the minor third "C" on the 6th string 8th fret. There will be a stretch in this shape from the 8th fret to the 12th fret and in this example we will use a bar an the 12th fret on the 6th and 5th strings. The picking remains the same: Up – Down – Down – Down – Down – Down – Down – Up (pull off) – Up – Up – Up – Up – Up – Down.

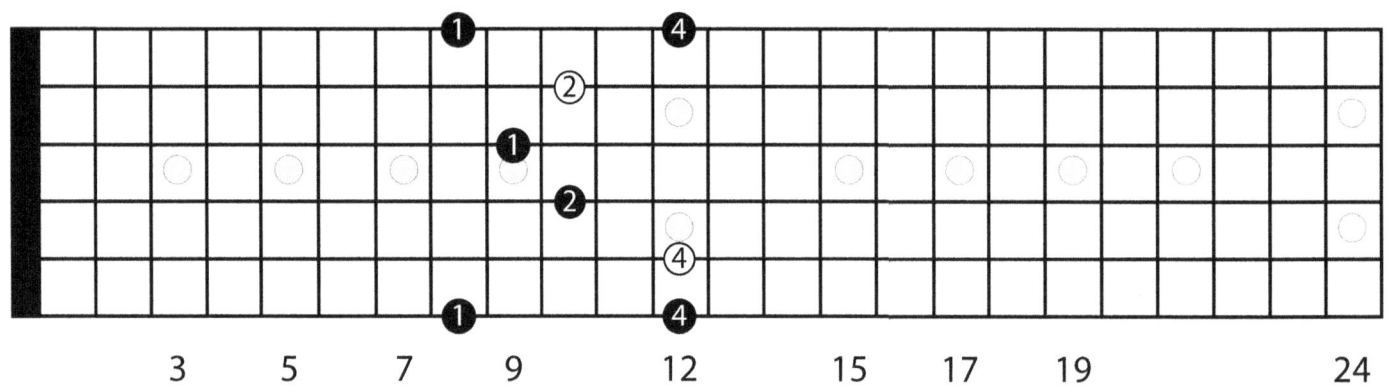

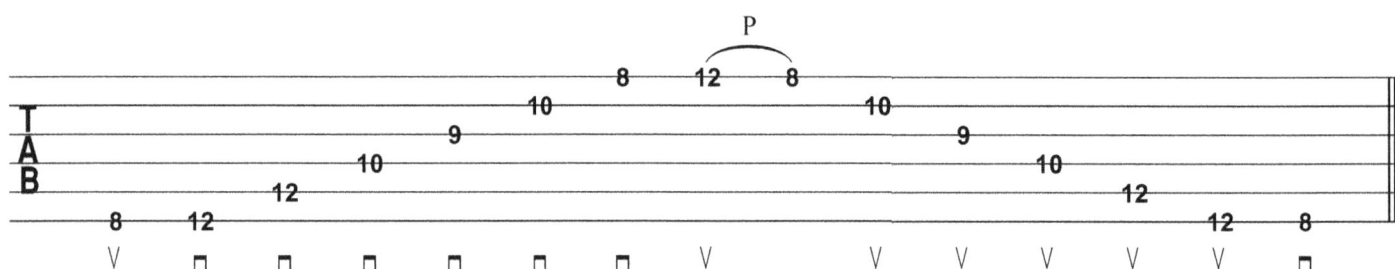

6-String Shape 2 – Derivative 1

The first derivative of the second shape is going to be played using strings 2 through five. The shape begins again on the minor third "C" on the 6th string 8th fret and will have a stretch on the 2nd string from the 8th fret to the 13th fret.

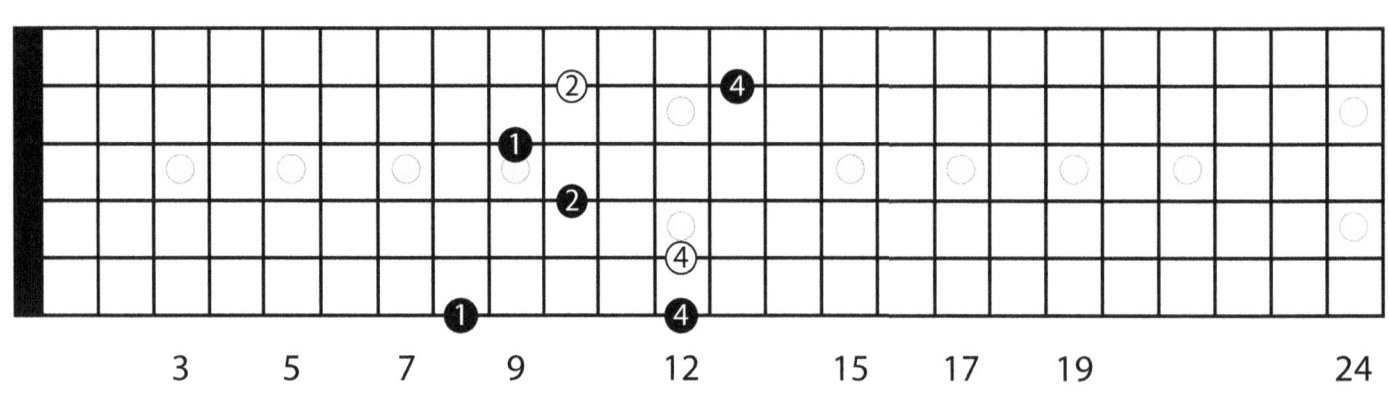

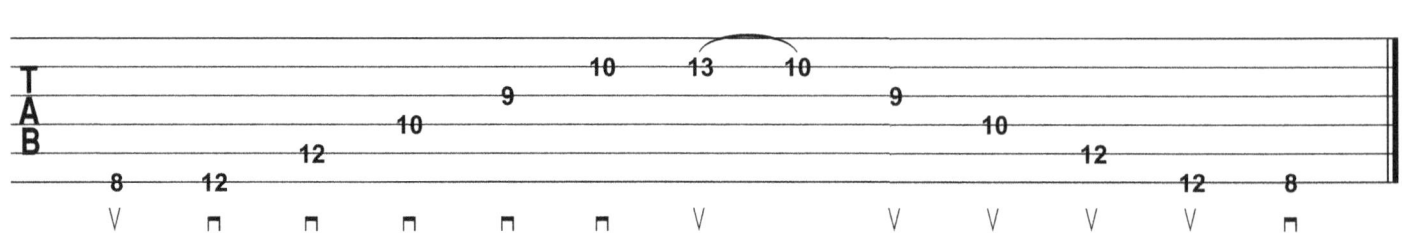

6-String Shape 2 – Derivative 2

The second derivative of the second shape is going to be played using strings one through five. This arpeggio is a second inversion because it begins on the fifth degree "E" on the 5th string 7th fret. There will be a stretch on the 1st and 5th strings from the 7th fret to the 12th fret.

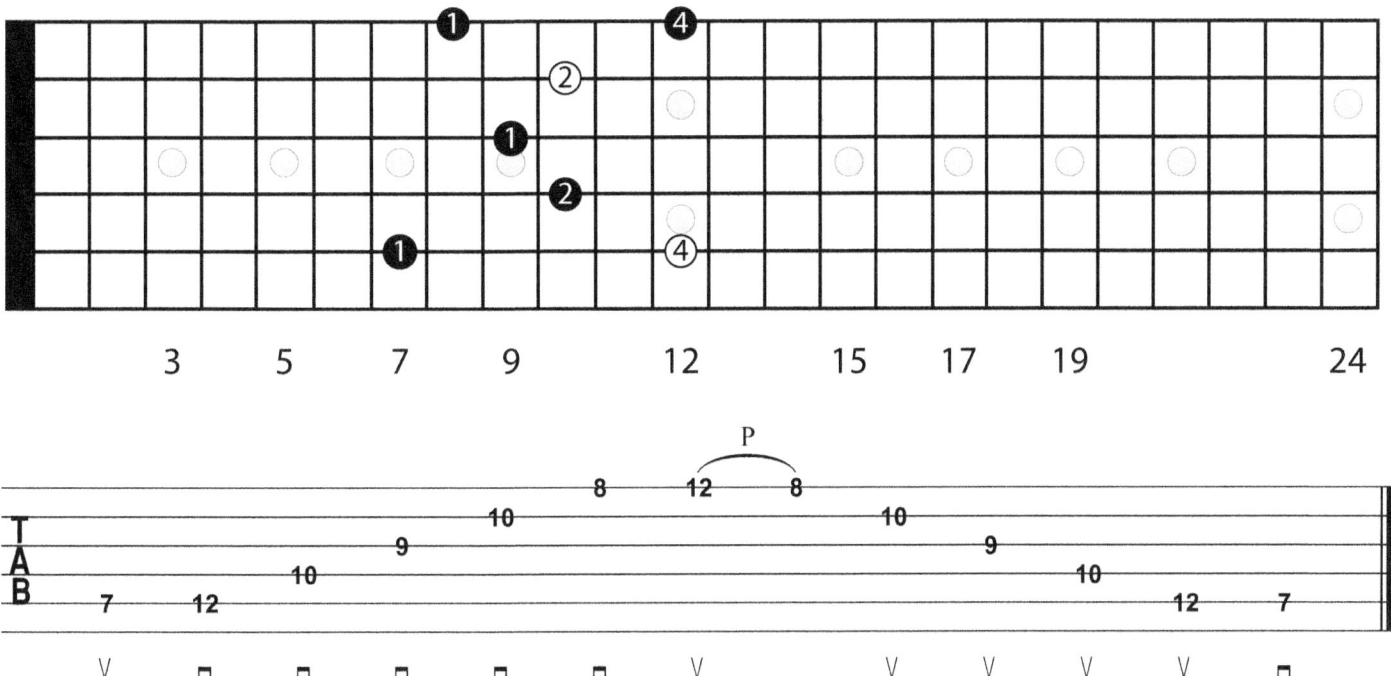

6-String Shape 3

The third shape is going to have a stretch from the 12th fret to the 17th fret on the 1st and 6th strings. However, because the frets are closer together the higher up the neck you travel, the stretch will not be too hard for your hands to accomplish with a little practice. This shape is once again a second inversion A minor arpeggio because it begins on the fifth "E." The part to really watch out for will be the cross over on between the 4th and 3rd strings where the 3rd finger plays the 14th fret 3rd string and the 2nd finger pays the 14th fret on the 4th string. Just like in the first derivative of shape 1, this will help articulate each note of the arpeggio.

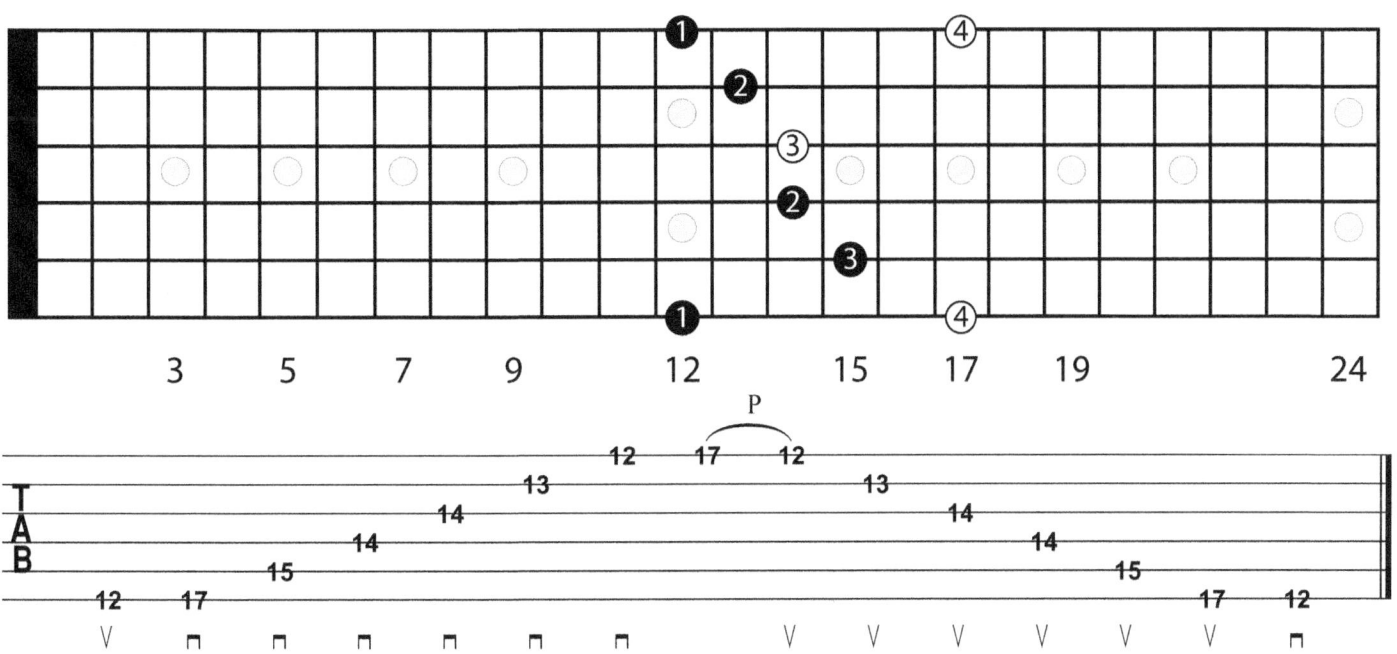

6-String Shape 2 – Derivative 1

Next is the first derivative for shape three. Once again this is a second inversion A minor arpeggio. In this example you have the stretch from the 12th to the 17th fret on the 6th string, and you also have a stretch from the 13th fret to the 17th fret on the 2nd string. However, this time you will use a second finger roll on the 4th and 3rd strings 14th fret.

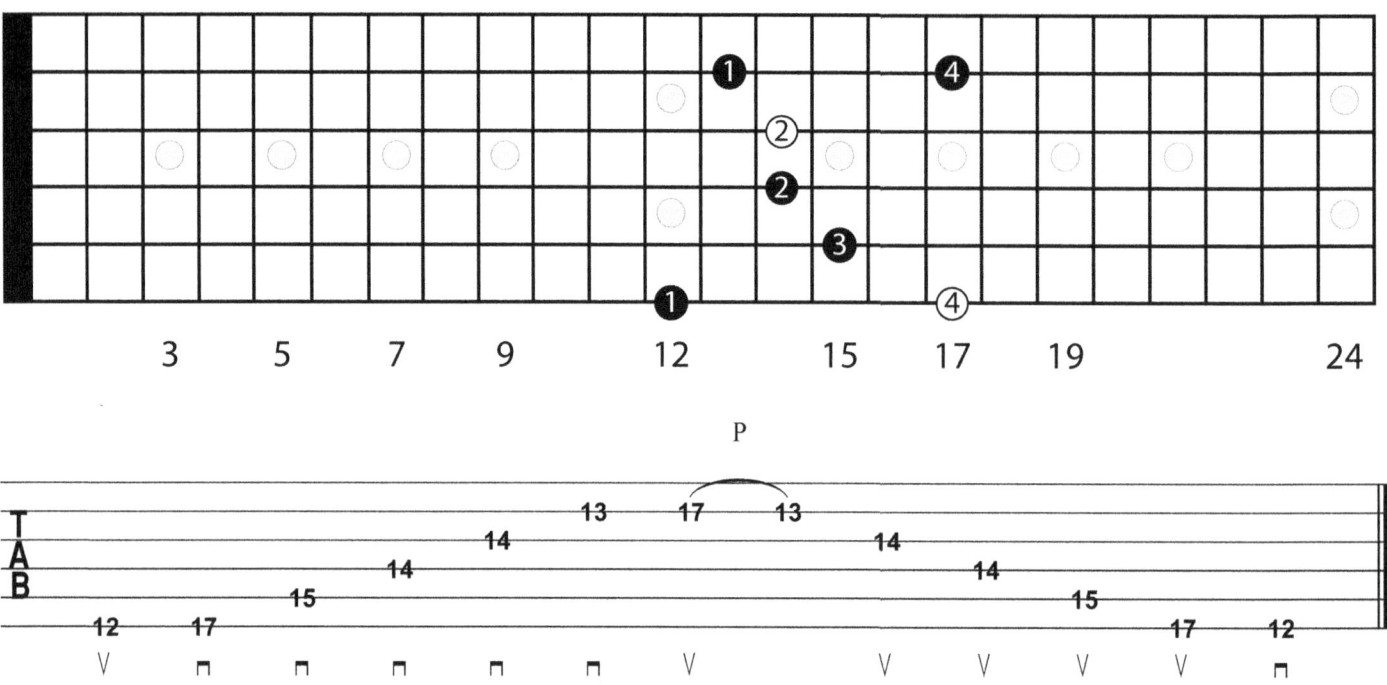

6-String Shape 3 – Derivative 2

The last A minor arpeggio shape for this chapter is a root position 5th string arpeggio. The biggest stretch in this arpeggio will occur on the 1st string between the 12th and 17th frets using your pinkie and index fingers. Also, there is a third finger roll on strings 4 and 3 on the 14th fret.

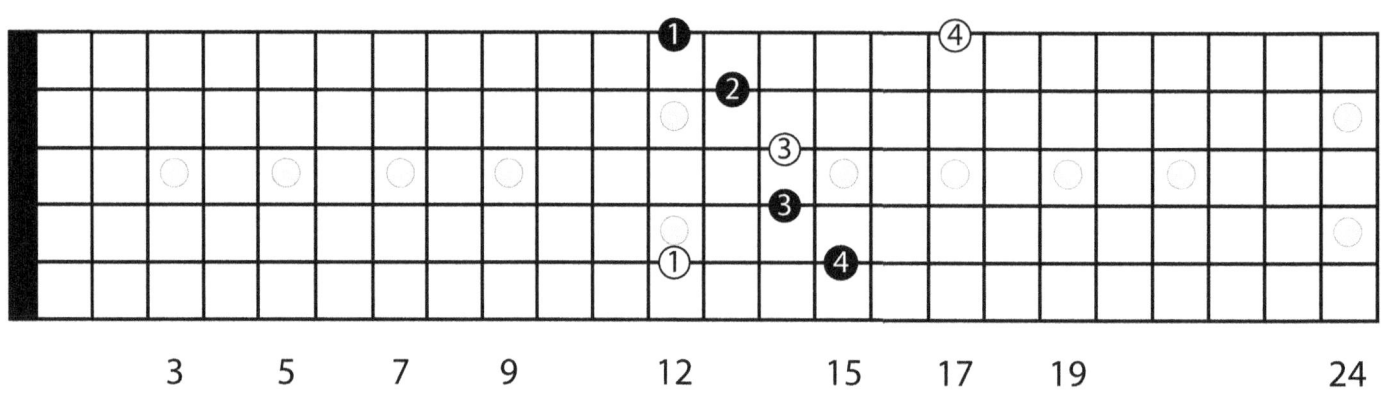

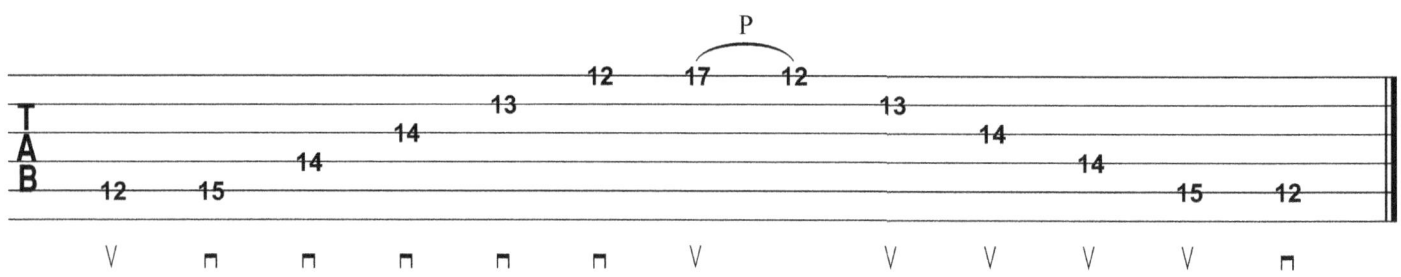

Chapter 2:
C Major Five & Six String Arpeggio Shapes

6-String C Major Shape 1

In this chapter we will be looking at some C Major 5 and 6 string arpeggio shapes as well as their derivatives just as we did in the last lesson, however, this time in a major setting. The major arpeggio formula is root - major third - perfect fifth. The picking will also be the same as the last lesson. The first arpeggio is a root position 6-string C major arpeggio beginning on the 8th fret of the 6th string. In this example you will have a stretch from the 8th to 12th frets on the 6th and 1st strings.

Notes: C - E - G Intervals: 1 3 5

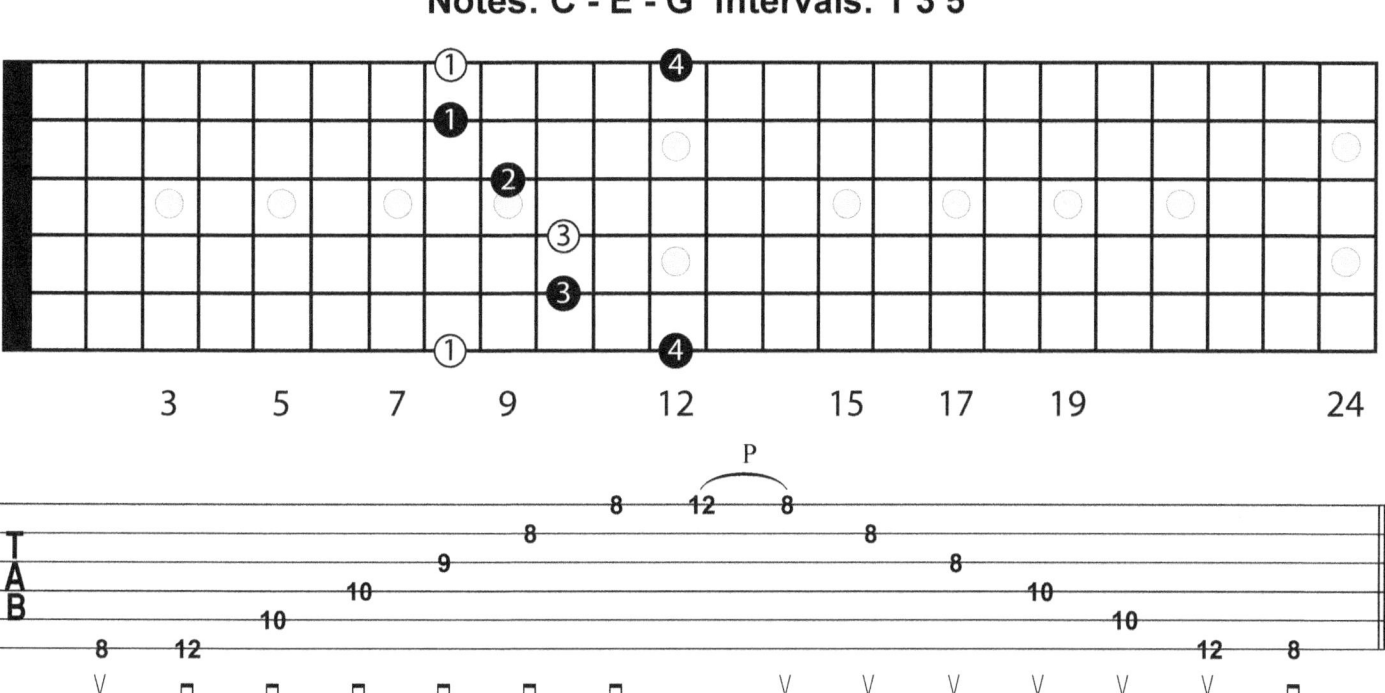

6-String C Major Shape 1 – Derivative 1

The first derivative is a 2-octave 5-string arpeggio beginning from the root note C. The shape begins on the 6th string 8th fret and plays up to the root note on the 2nd string 13th fret. There will be a third finger roll on the 5th and 4th strings at the 10th fret.

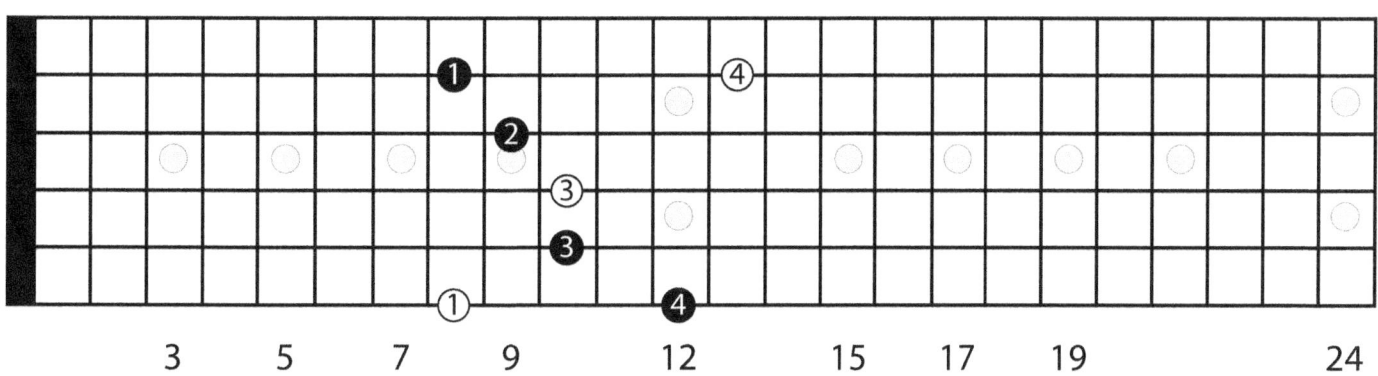

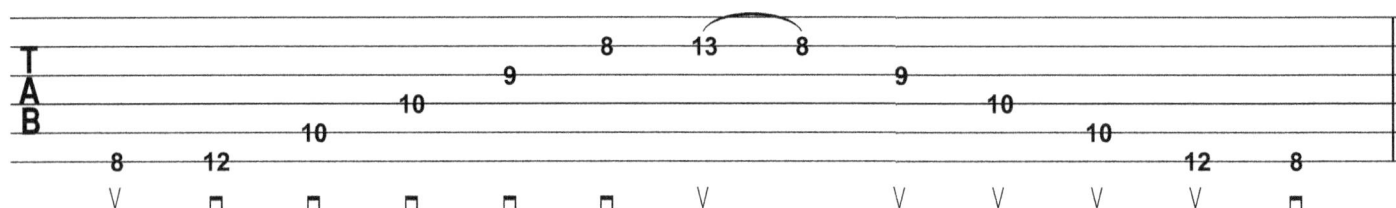

6-String C Major Shape 1 – Derivative 2

The second derivative is a 2-octave 5 string first inversion C major arpeggio. The shape begins on the major third "E" on the 5th string 7th fret. There will be a 3rd finger roll on the 5th and 4th strings at the 10th fret as well.

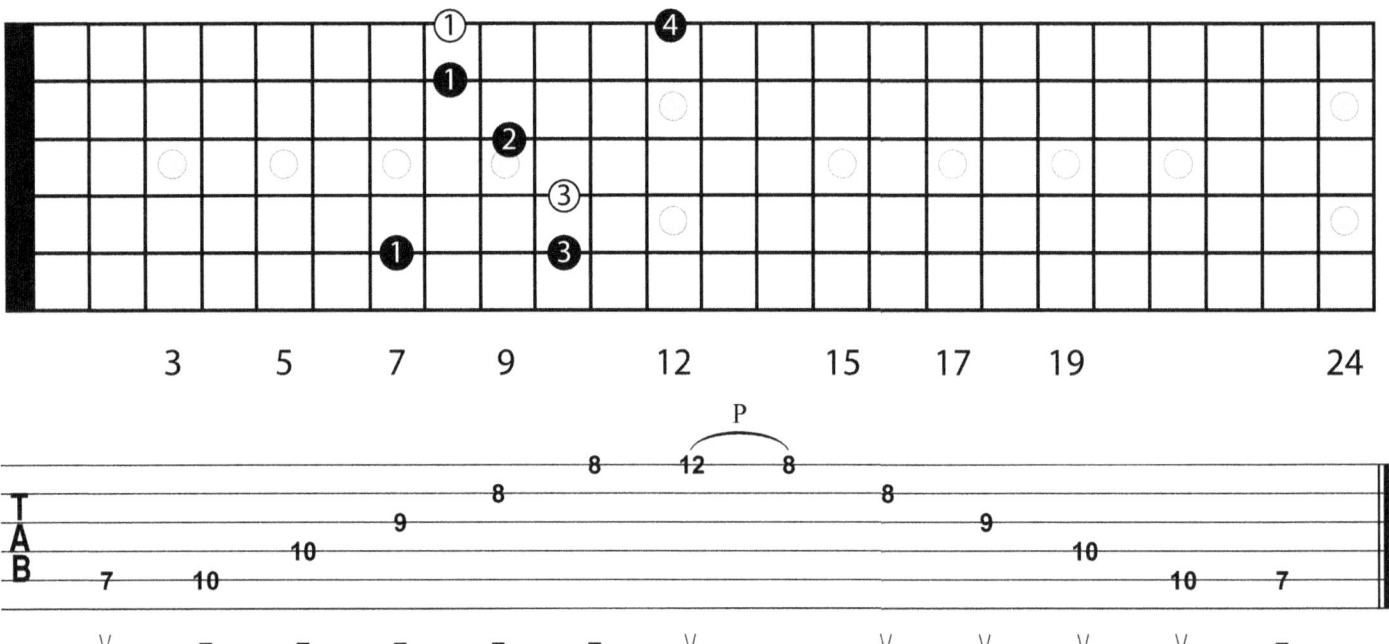

6-String C Major Shape 2

The Second C major arpeggio shape begins on the third degree E making this a first inversion arpeggio. Watch out for the 4th finger roll on strings 6 and 5 at the 15th fret and make sure the notes are played clearly through this example:

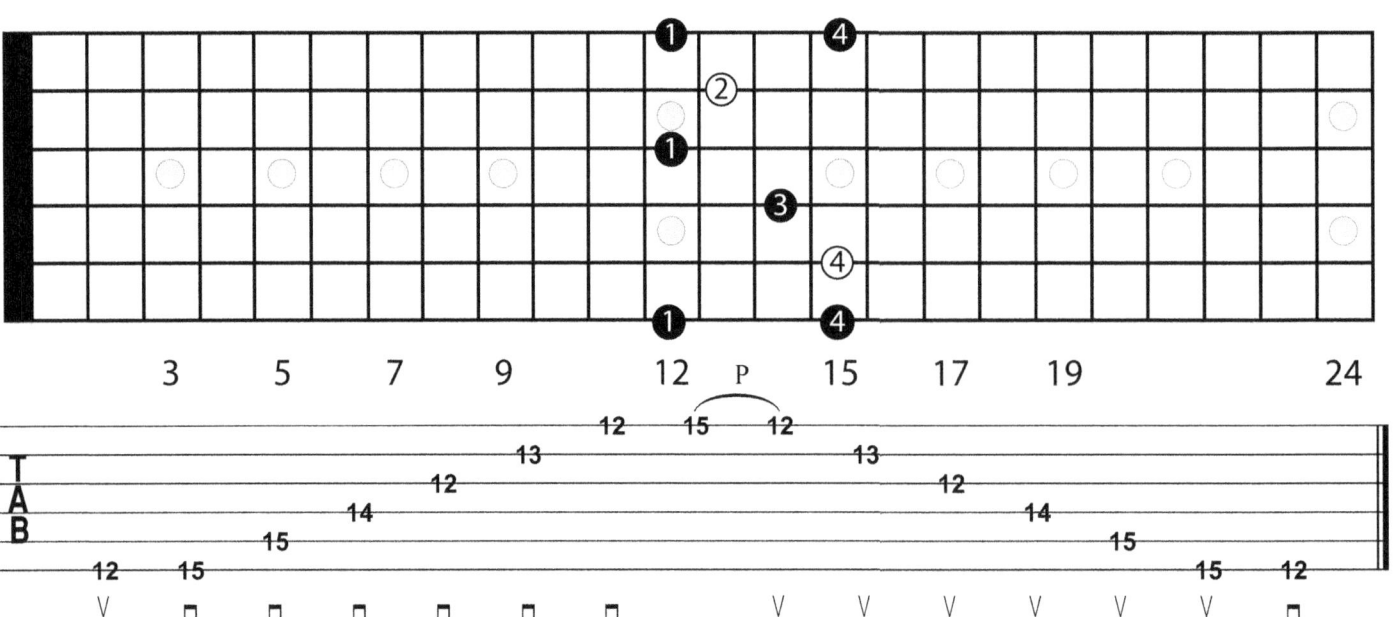

6-String C Major Shape 2 – Derivative 1

The first derivative of the second C major shape spans from string 2 through 6 and is a first inversion arpeggio. In this example you still have the 4th finger roll as before but there is an added stretch from the 13th fret to the 17th fret using your 2nd and 4th fingers.

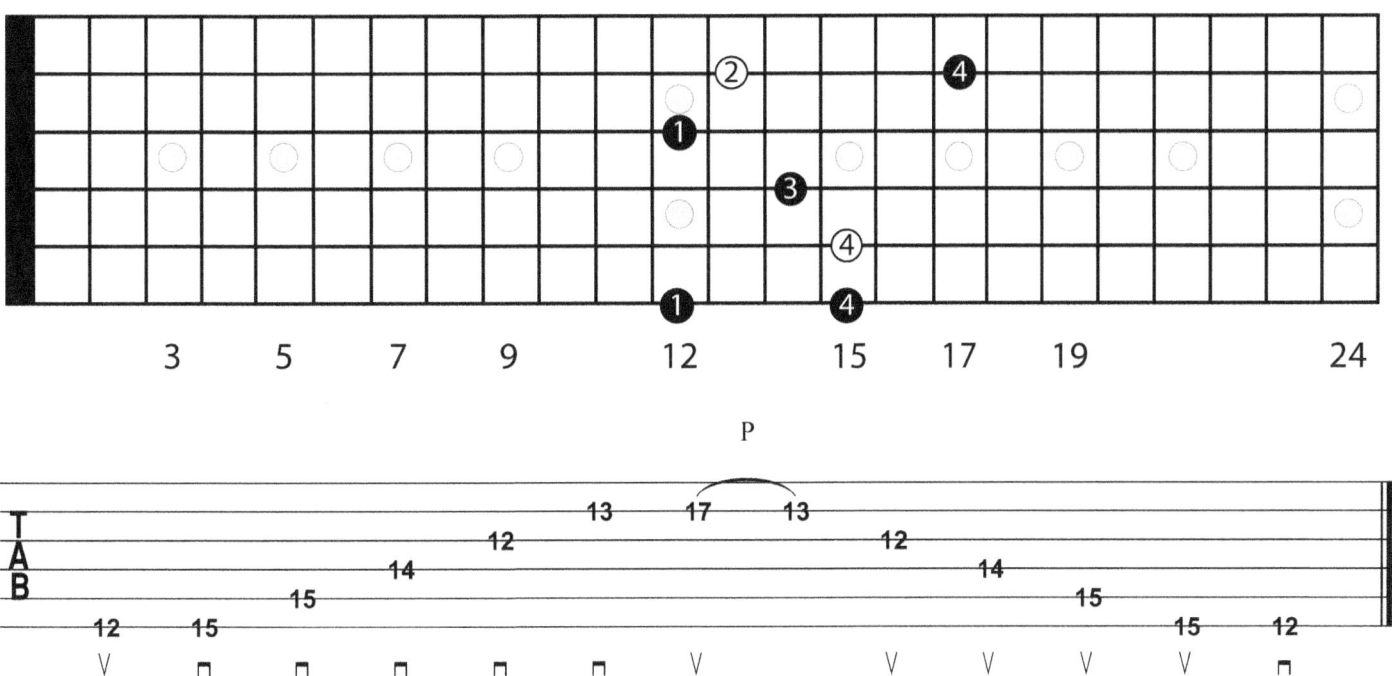

6-String C Major Shape 2 – Derivative 2

The second derivative of shape two has a sizeable stretch to begin. The pattern begins on the 5th string 10th fret with your 1st finger and stretches up to the 15th fret with your pinkie. This will be the trickiest part of this arpeggio. If you find any kind of trouble trying to play this part, ascend and descend the first three notes of the pattern repeatedly until it becomes easier. As you play through this shape, keep the notes clean, crisp and articulate. This shape is also a favorite of Rusty's because there is no bar within the pattern.

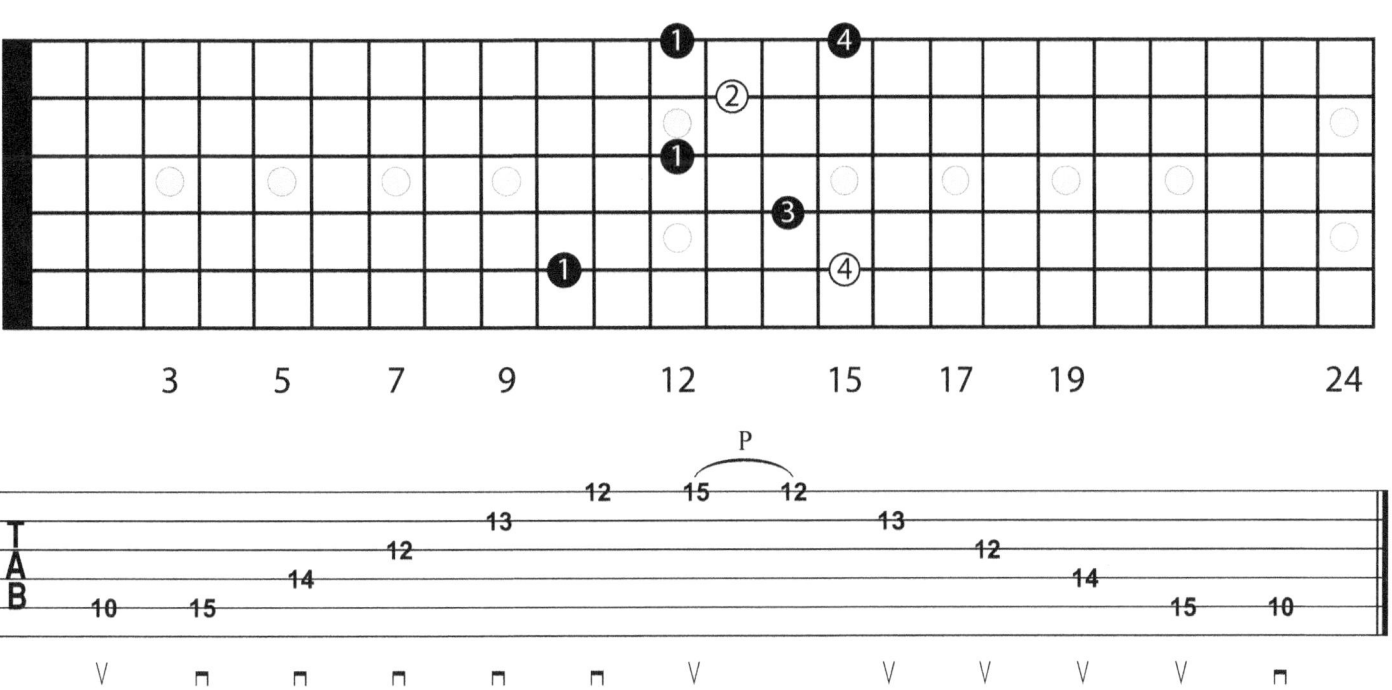

6-String C Major Shape 3

The third C major arpeggio shape will use all six strings and begins on the 15th fret of the 6th string with a slight stretch to the 20th fret. The section that requires the most attention in this shape is the three-string rolling bar on the 4th, 3rd and 2nd strings at the 17th fret with your 2nd finger.

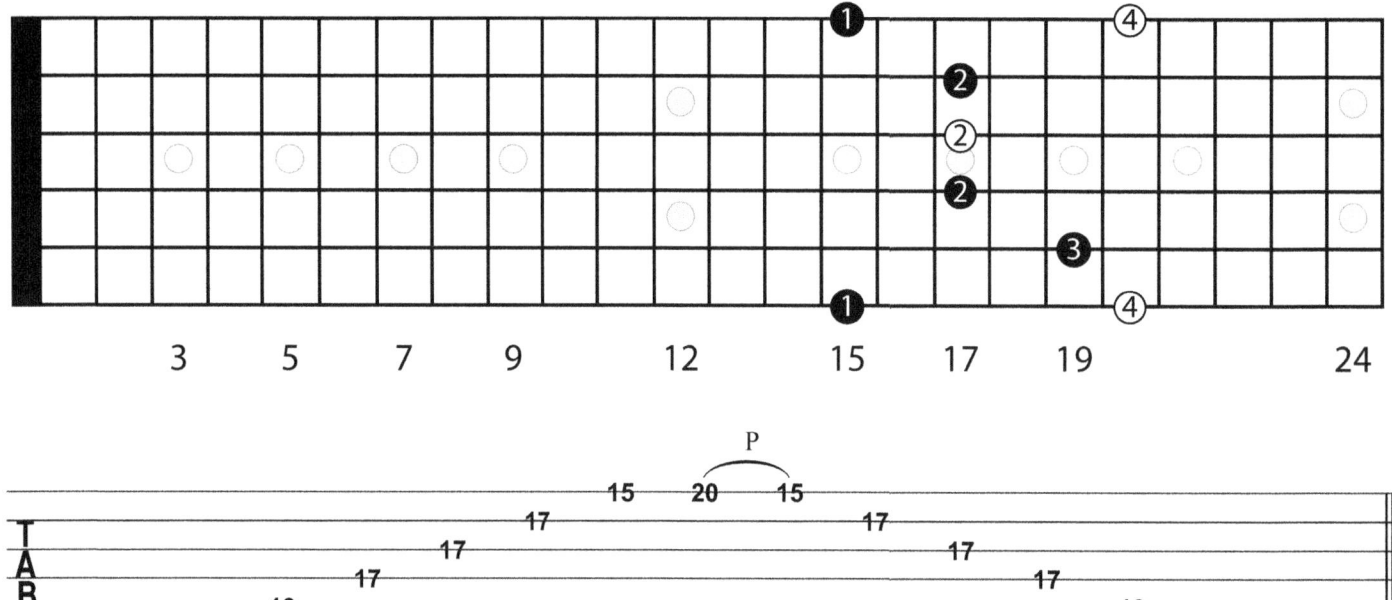

6-String C Major Shape 3 – Derivative 1

The first derivative is very similar to the third 6-string C major shape; you still have the three string finger roll as before, however, this time instead of playing the bar with your 2nd finger you will use your 1st finger.

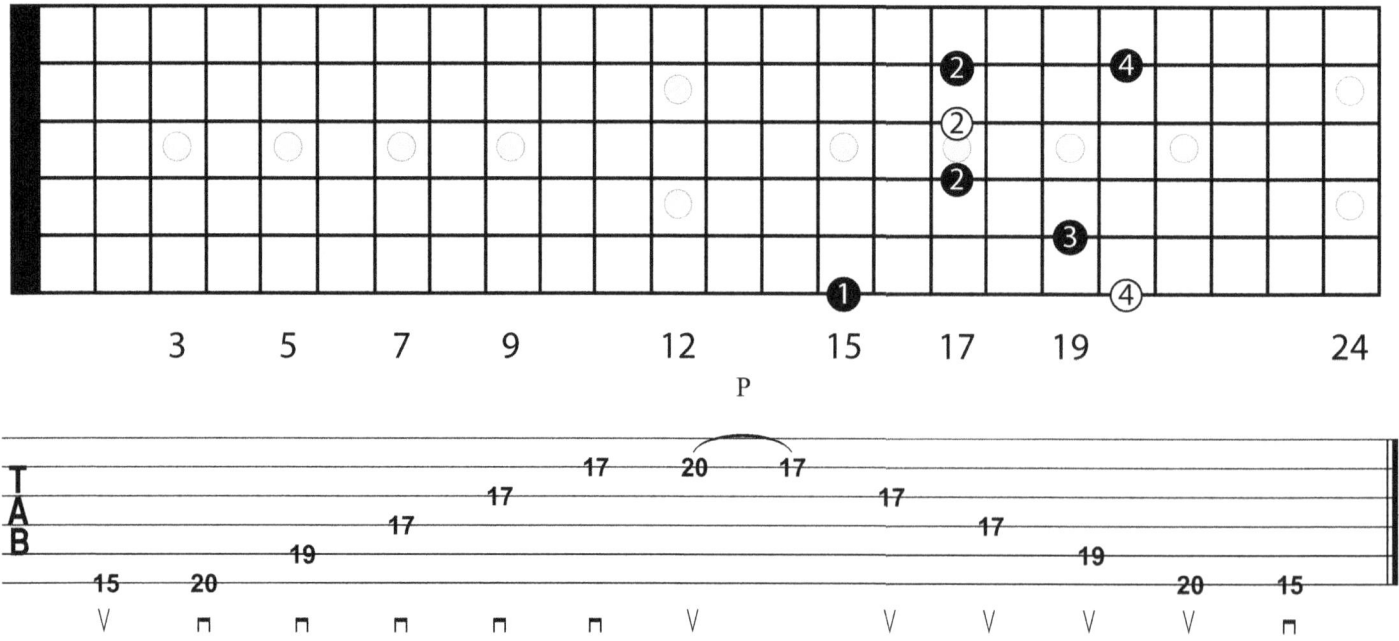

6-String C Major Shape 3 – Derivative 2

The second derivative is another 5 string, two-octave arpeggio using strings 1 through 5. This pattern begins on the root note "C" and ends on the high "C" note on the 1st string 20th fret.

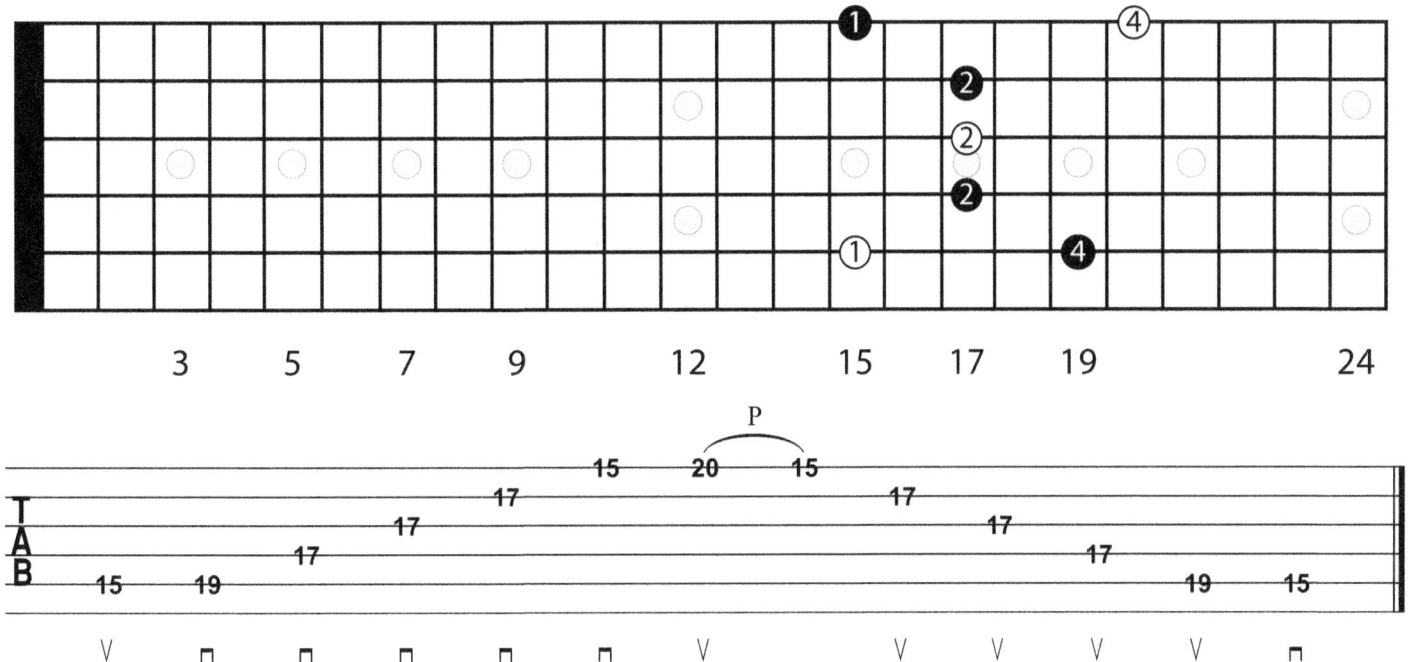

Chapter 3:
B Diminished Arpeggios

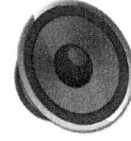

6-String B Diminished Shape 1

Now lets look at some B diminished arpeggios. The formula for the diminished arpeggio is root - minor third - diminished fifth.

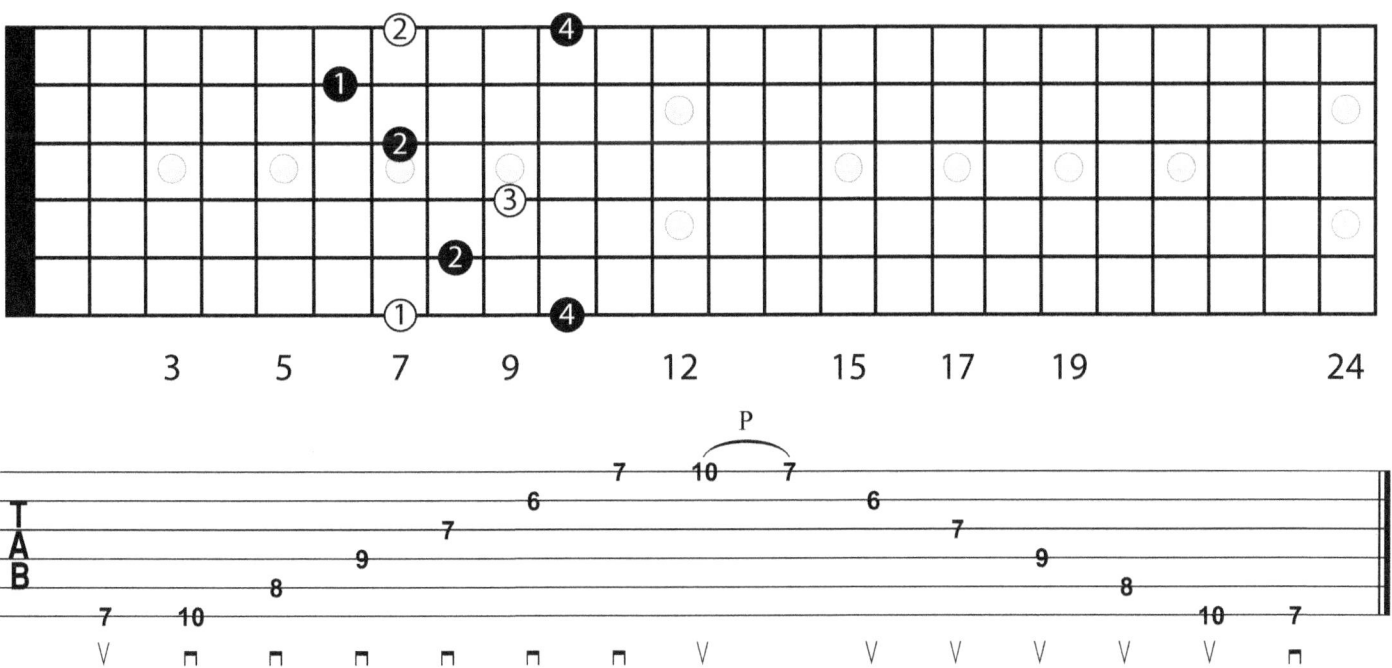

19

6-String B Diminished Shape 1 – Derivative 1

The first derivative is another two-octave arpeggio shape that begins in the same position as the six-string shape 1 pattern; however, this is a five string derivative and is also a stretch from the 6th fret to the 12th fret on the 2nd string.

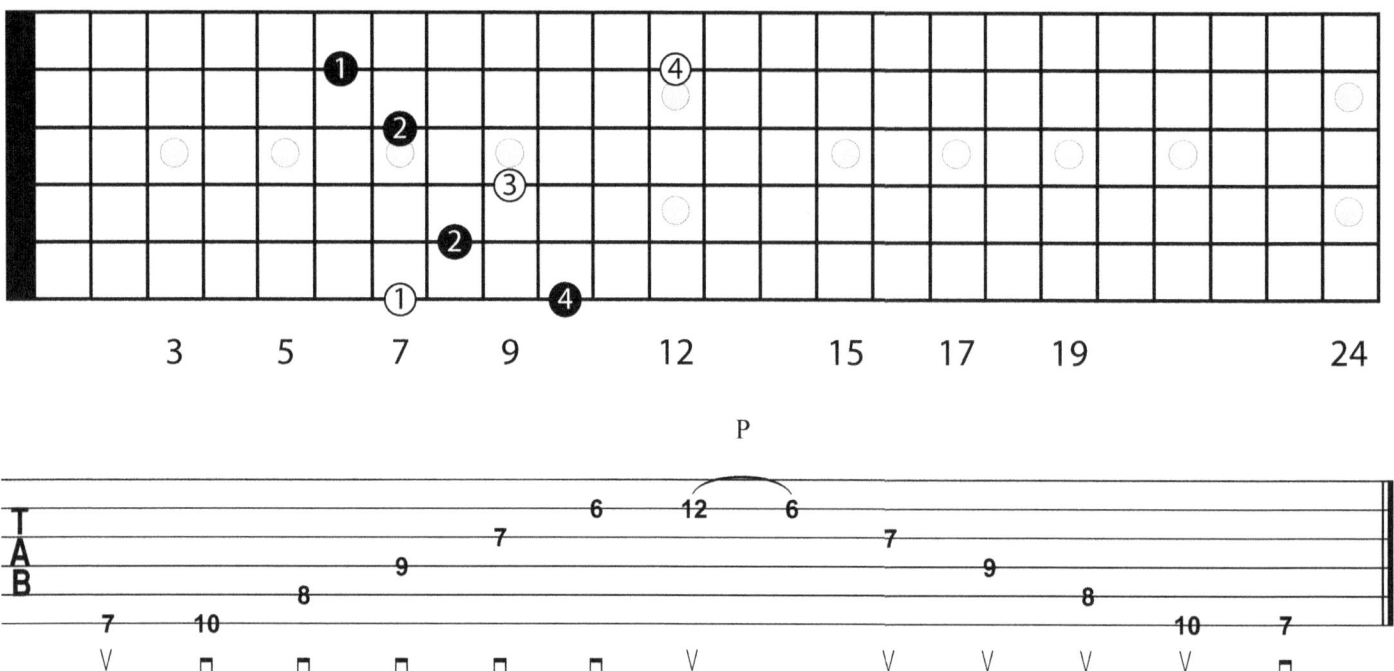

6-String B Diminished Shape 1 – Derivative 2

Next is the second derivative of the B diminished shape. This is another five-string shape that employs a big stretch from the 8th to the 14th frets. This is a second inversion arpeggio beginning on the diminished fifth "F."

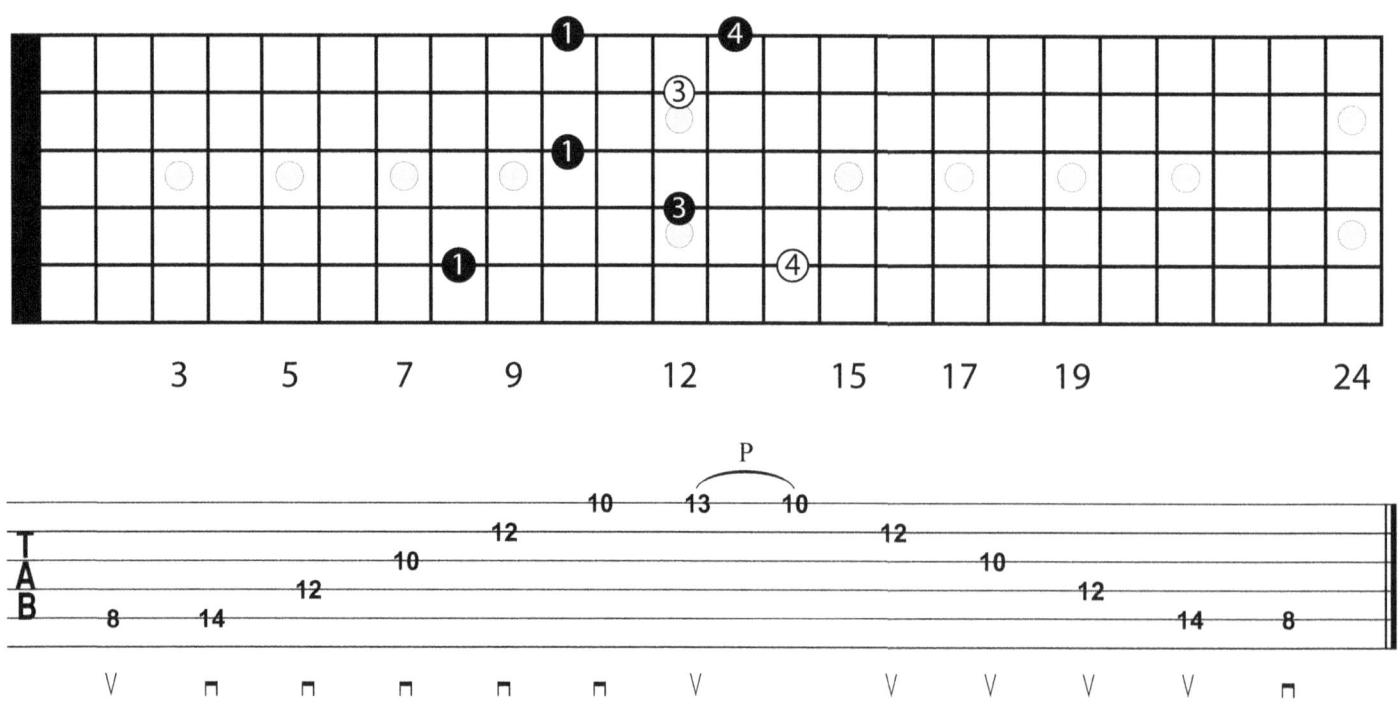

6-String B Diminished Shape 2

The second six-string shape is another second inversion two-octave arpeggio that begins on "F" at the 13th fret of the 6th string. There will be two stretches from the 12th to the 19th fret on both the 1st and 6th strings.

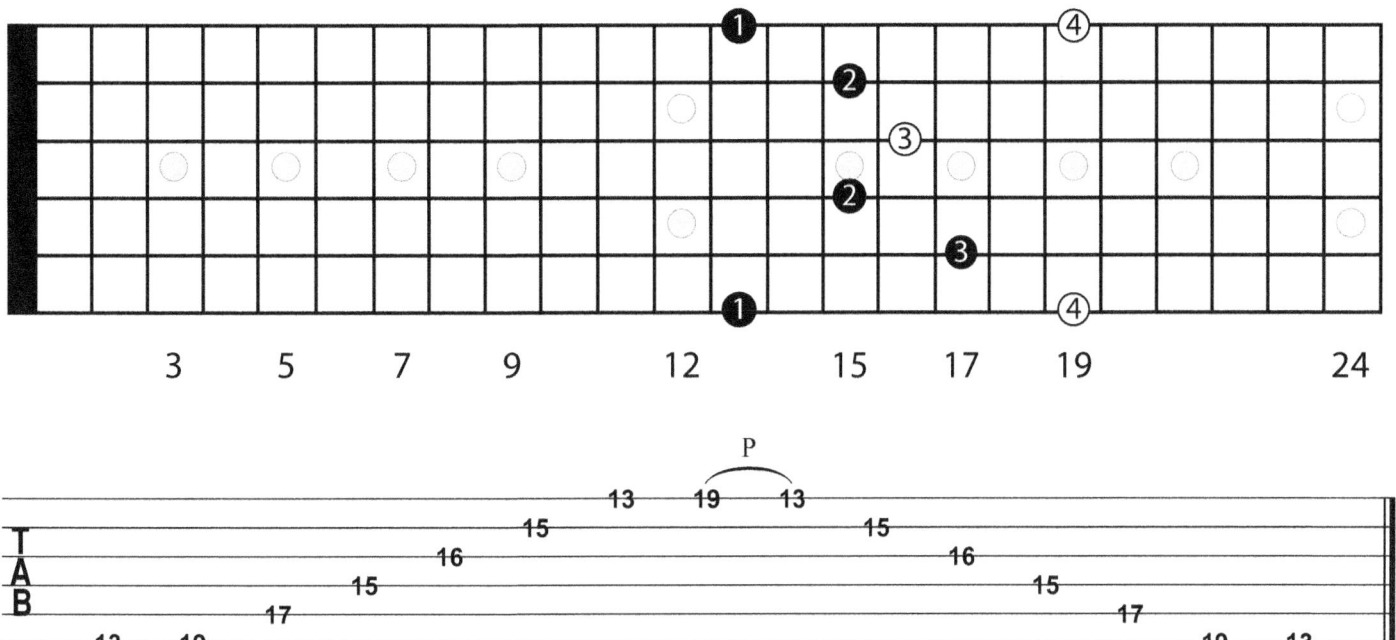

6-String B Diminished Shape 2 – Derivative 1

The first derivative is a five-string second-inversion pattern that again begins on the 6th string 13th fret and will end on the 2nd string 18th fret.

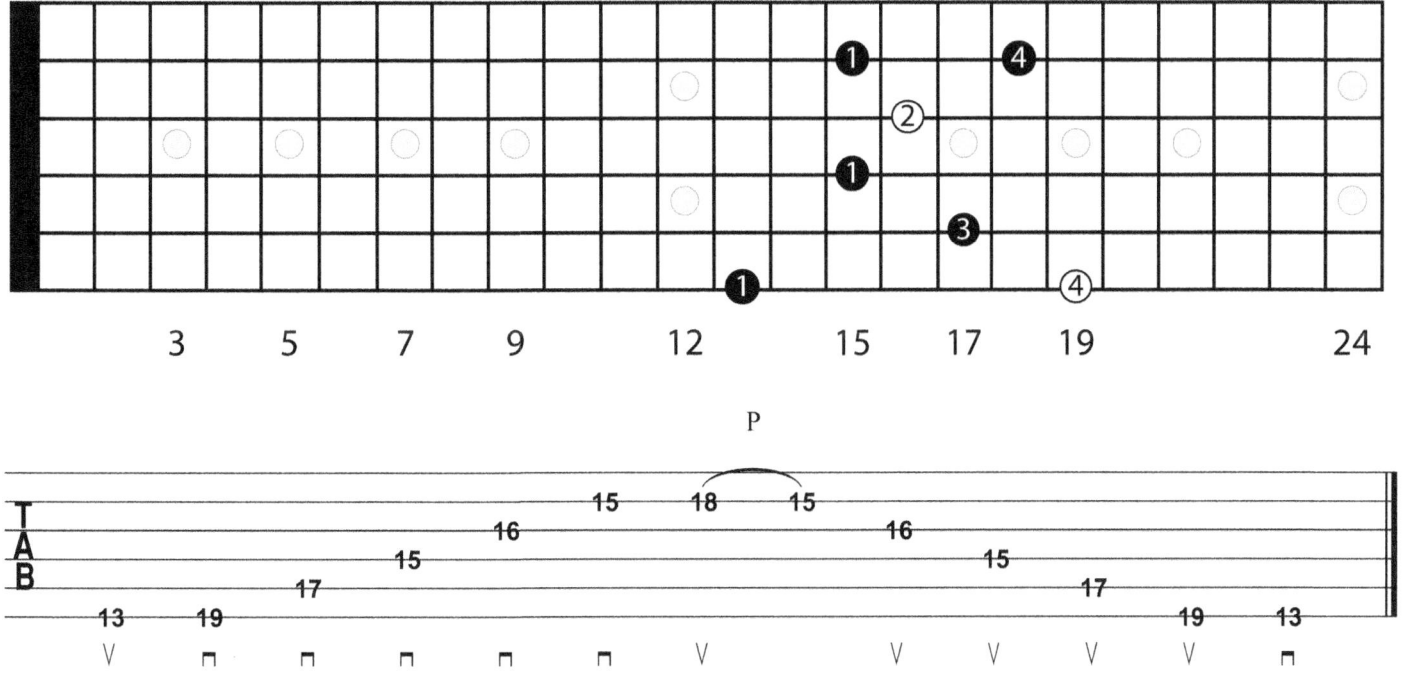

6-String B Diminished Shape 2 – Derivative 2

The last derivative is a root fifth two-octave arpeggio that begins at the 14th fret of the fifth string and ends on the B note on the 1st string 19th fret.

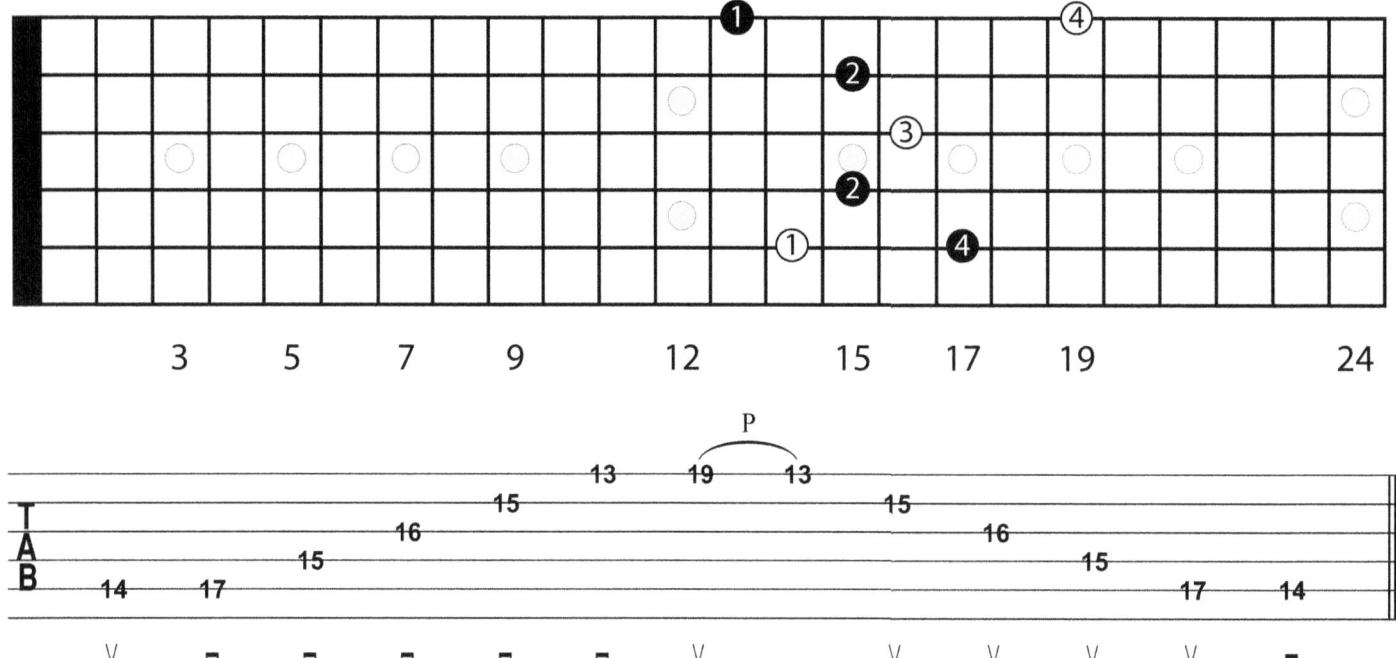

Chapter 4:
Three to Five String Arpeggio Sequences

In this chapter we are going to cover eight arpeggio sequences that utilize some of the shapes we just learned as well as some new shapes. Rusty calls these "Three to Five String Sequences" because they start with a sweep of the first three strings, then use strings one through five on the repeat. These arpeggios are very reminiscent of the way Jason Becker a hero of Rusty's sequenced arpeggios.

The first arpeggio is going to be an E minor arpeggio (root-minor third - perfect fifth) based on the **6-string shape 2 - second derivative minor** arpeggio shape we covered earlier in the book. You will play the first three strings descending then ascending, on the repeat of the descend you will play all the way to the 5th string 14th fret before ascending back to the high E string. The picking for these arpeggios will be: Down - Up - Up - Up - Down - Down - Up (pull-off) - Up - Up - Up - Up - Down (hammer-on) - Down - Down - Down - Down - Down.

Notes: E - G - B Intervals: 1 b3 5

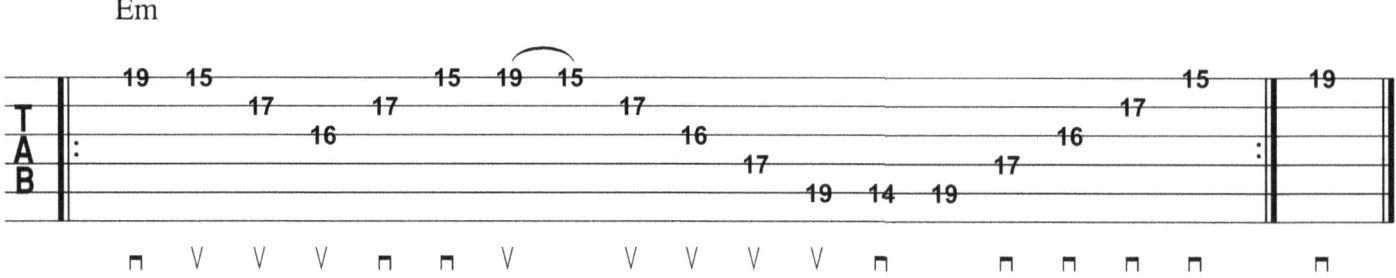

The next arpeggio is three to five string C major arpeggio (root - major third - perfect fifth). This sequence is based off of the **C major 6-string shape 2 - second derivative** covered in chapter 2. The picking pattern and sequencing concept remain the same throughout this and the rest of the arpeggios in this chapter.

Notes: C - E - G Intervals: 1 3 5

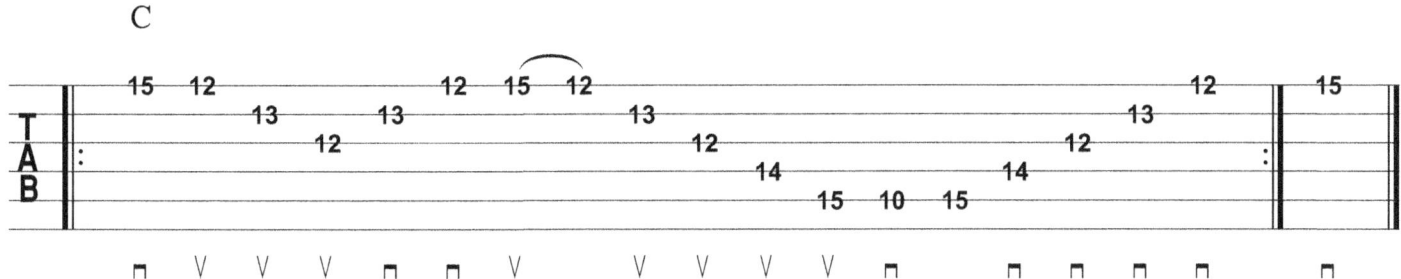

Next is a B diminished arpeggio (root - minor third - diminished fifth) and is based on the **B Diminished 6-string shape 1 - second derivative** arpeggio we covered in chapter 3.

Notes: B - D - F Intervals: 1 b3 b5

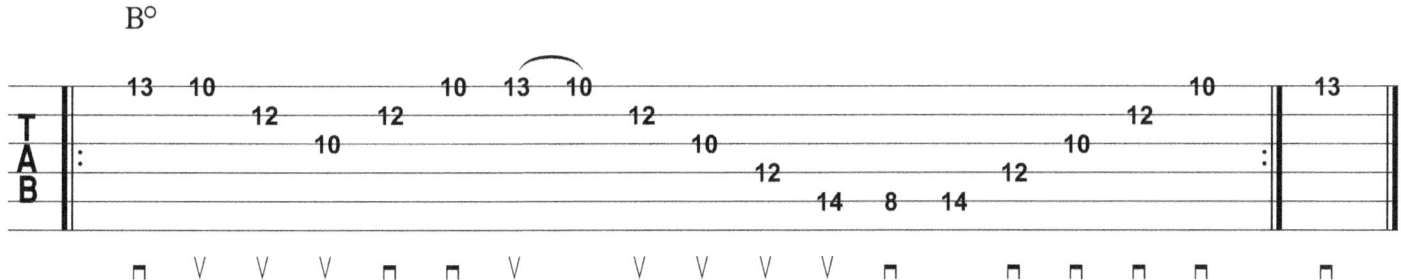

Now lets look at a new arpeggio, the augmented arpeggio that consists of the intervals: root - major third - augmented (sharped) fifth. From C, these notes will be C - E - G#. The arpeggio begins on the augmented fifth G# and travels via the sequence down to octaves to the G# at the 11th fret on the 5th string. The augmented arpeggio can be visualized as a major arpeggio with a raised fifth degree. So if you look at the **6-String Shape 2 - derivative 2** C major arpeggio in chapter 2, and just raise the G notes to G# you will see how this arpeggio lines up to that which you already learned.

Notes: C - E - G# Intervals: 1 3 #5

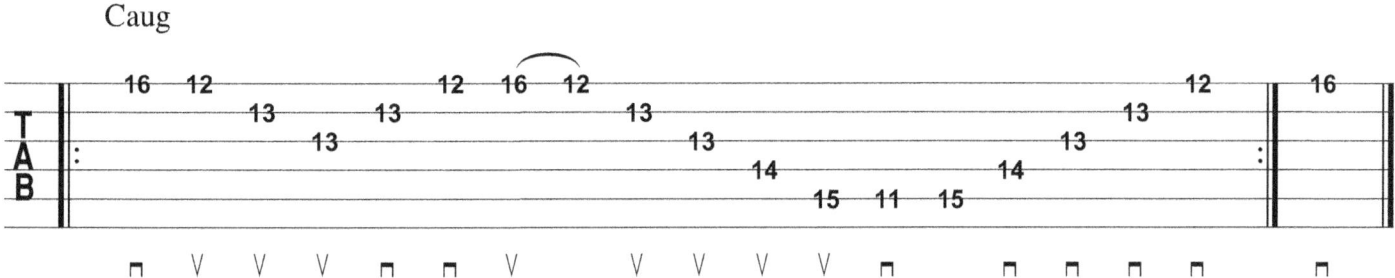

The next example is another A minor sequence. This time the sequence is based off of the A minor **6-String Shape 3 - derivative 2** shape we learned at the end of the first chapter.

Notes: A - C - E Intervals: 1 ♭3 5

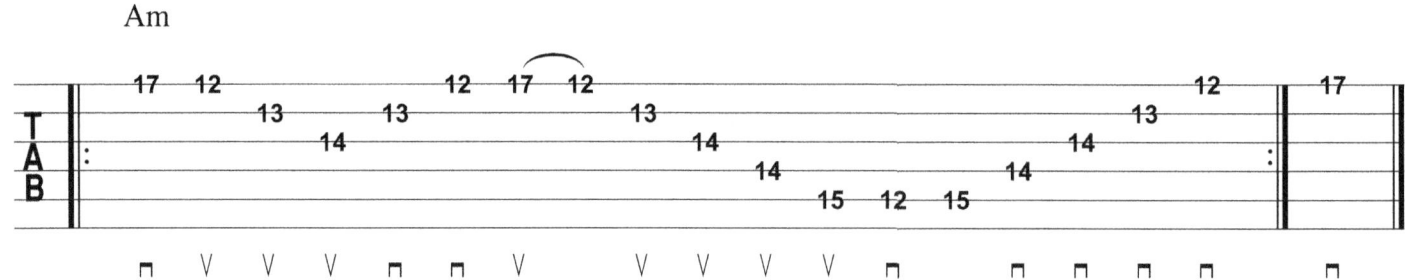

Here is another major arpeggio. This time we will shift the **C major 6-string Shape 3 - derivative 2** shape from Chapter 2 down two frets to play a Bb major five string arpeggio.

Notes: B♭ - D - F Intervals: 1 3 5

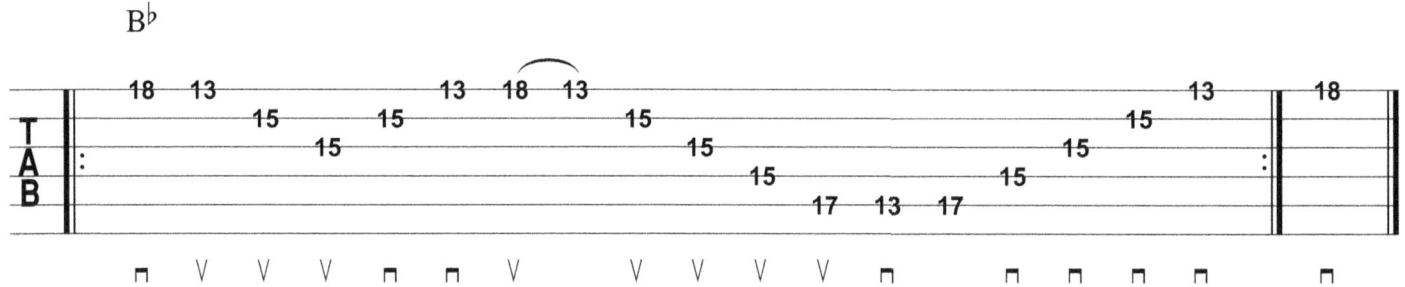

Now lets explore another diminished arpeggio. This example is based off of the **B Diminished 6-String Shape 2** - derivative 2.

Notes: B - D - F Intervals: 1 ♭3 ♭5

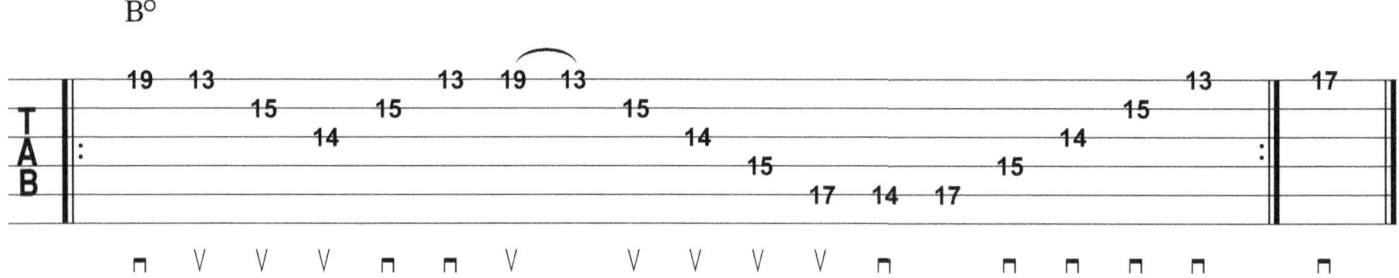

The last three to five string sequence we are going to cover is another C augmented arpeggio. This time we have a **C major 6-string Shape 3 - derivative 2** arpeggio with the fifths raised from G to G♯.

Notes: C - E - G♯ Intervals: 1 3 ♯5

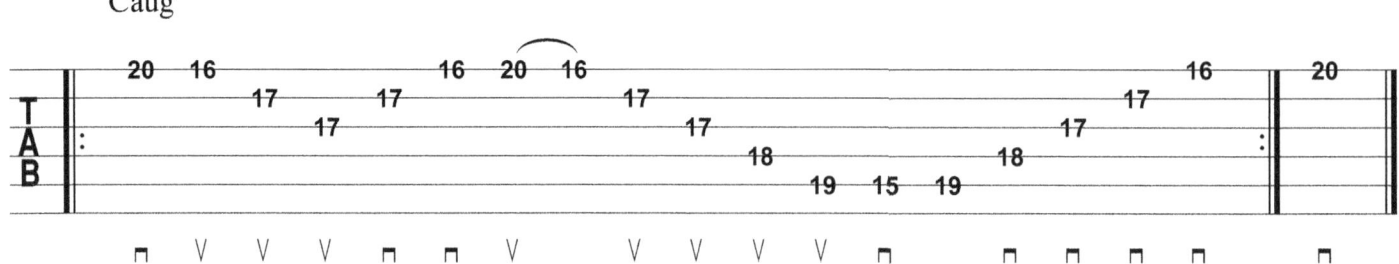

24

Chapter 5:
Melodic Arpeggios

In this chapter we will explore melodic arpeggios that have added diatonic notes. Diatonic notes are notes that belong to a key. For example, in the key of E minor we have the notes:

E - F♯ - G - A - B - C - D - E

R - 2 - ♭3 - 4 - 5 - ♭6 - ♭7 - 8/Oct.

In the E minor arpeggio we have the notes E - G - B, which are the root, minor third and perfect fifth. So the remaining four notes F♯, A, C and D are diatonic notes because they come from the E minor scale and are not used within the basic E minor triad. Rusty will add these other diatonic notes at will without really paying much mind to what notes he's actually adding in because he knows that they are all diatonic to the key of E minor. When these other diatonic notes are added in they give the arpeggio a more melodic sound.

In the first example, Rusty takes the E minor three string arpeggio and adds in the F♯ at the 14th fret (the second degree) and the minor sixth C on the 1st string 20th fret.

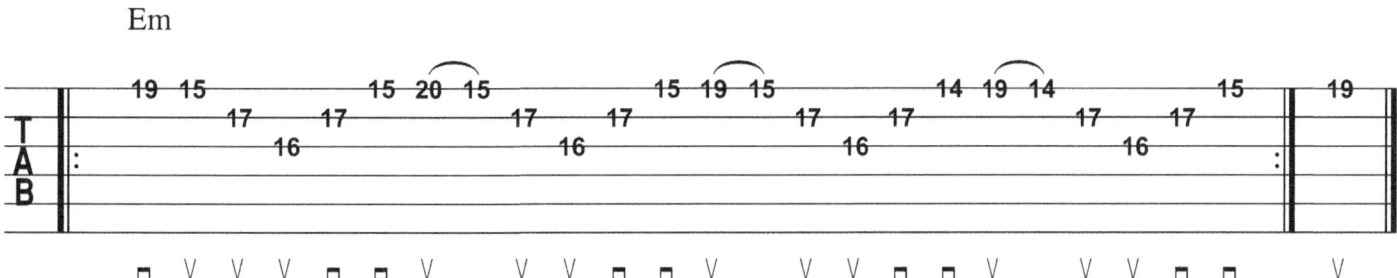

The next example is an A minor arpeggio derived from the E minor scale. In the context of the E minor scale, A minor functions as the two chord which is derived from the Dorian mode, in this case the A Dorian mode. The A Dorian mode has the intervallic structure: root - major second - minor third - perfect fourth - perfect fifth - major sixth and minor seventh (A - B - C - D - E - F♯ - G - A). In this example Rusty adds to the A minor triad: F♯ the major sixth at the 14th fret of the 1st string as well as the major second B at the 7th fret of the 1st string. The picking and sequential pattern will remain the same as before in the E minor arpeggio we just covered.

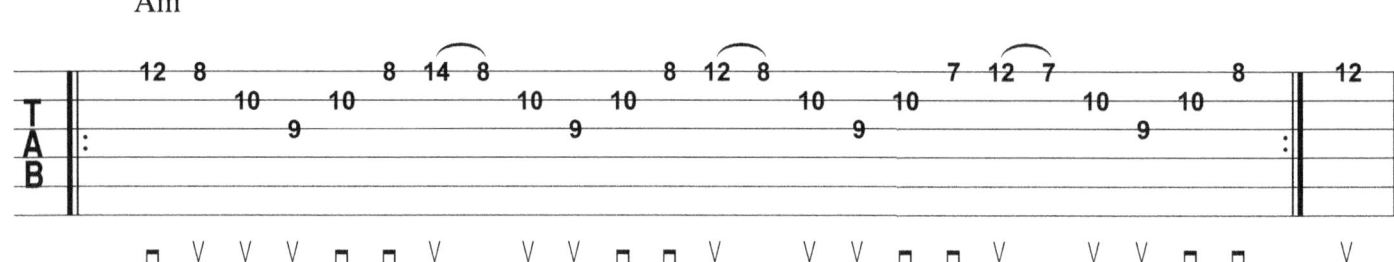

Next up is a B minor arpeggio. In this example the extension notes will be taken from the B Phrygian minor mode. the fifth mode of the E minor scale:

B - C - D - E - F♯ - G - A - B
R - ♭2 - ♭3 - 4 - 5 - ♭6 - ♭7 - 8/Oct.

The extensions Rusty uses are the minor 6th G on the 15th fret of the 1st string and the minor second C on the 8th fret of the 1st string. It is important to understand that the minor second C note gives the Phrygian mode it's unique sound characteristic.

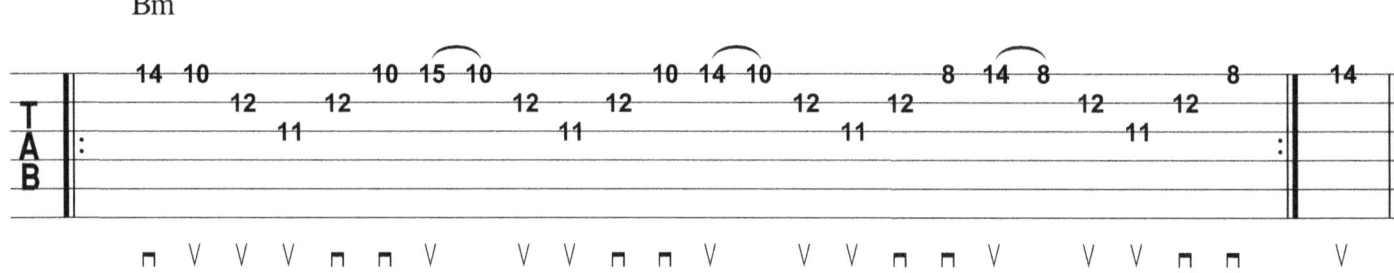

Now lets look at a G major arpeggio sequence. G major is the relative major of E minor and its structure is as follows:

G - A - B - C - D - E - F♯ - G
R - 2 - 3 - 4 - 5 - 6 - 7 - 8/Oct.

The extensions in this sequence will be the major 6th E on the 1st string 24th fret and the major second A on the 1st string 17th fret.

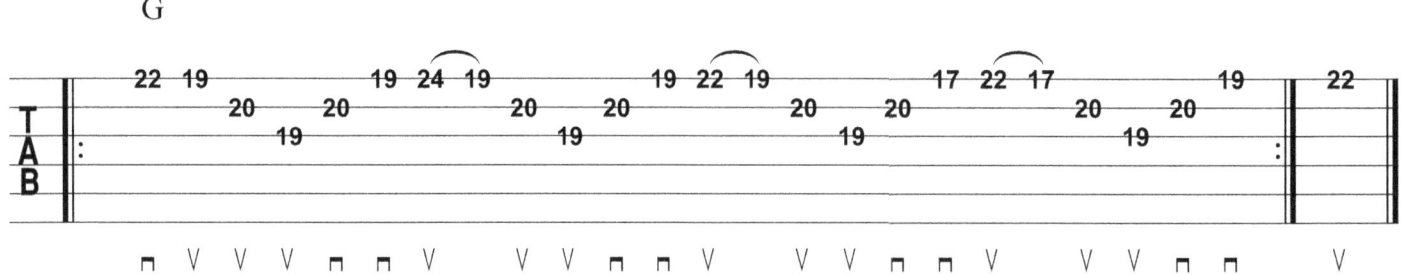

The following melodic arpeggio sequence is based on the seventh mode of the E minor scale; D Mixolydian mode. The structure for this mode is:

D - E - F♯ - G - A - B - C - D

R - 2 - 3 - 4 - 5 - 6 - ♭7 - 8/Oct.

One way a lot of players look at this mode is as a Major scale with a minor (flatted) seventh degree. The extensions Rusty uses from this mode are the major sixth B on the 1st string 19th fret and the major second E on the 1st string 12th fret.

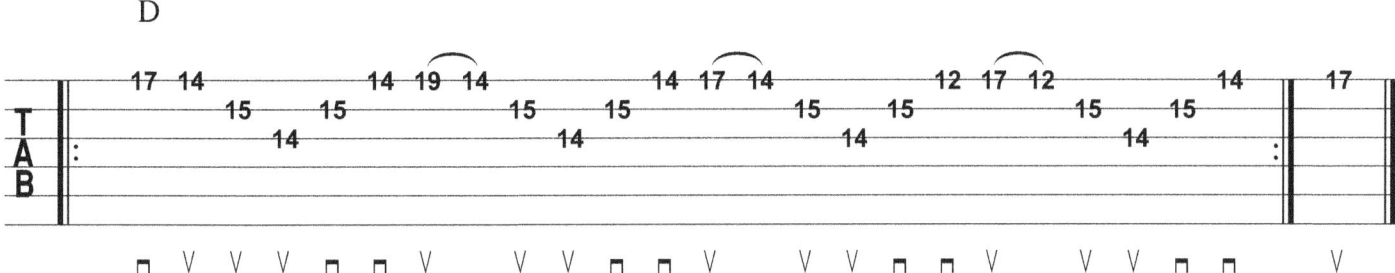

In this next example we are going to use a C major arpeggio, with extensions from the C Lydian major mode; the 6th mode of E minor:

C - D - E - F♯ - G - A - B - C

R - 2 - 3 - ♯4 - 5 - 6 - 7 - 8/Oct.

In this example the extensions will be the major sixth degree A at the 17th fret of the 1st string, and the major second D at the 10th fret of the 1st string. I also think that it is important to realize, that though it's not apparent in this example, you should be aware that the unique sound of this mode comes from the augmented fourth (♯4) degree.

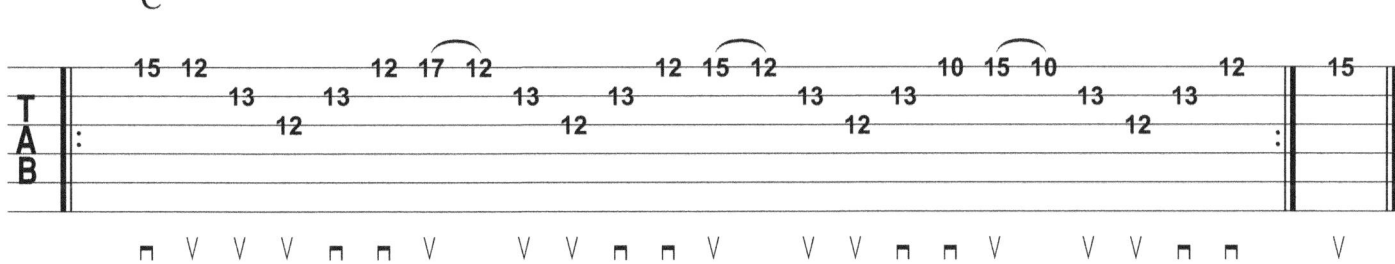

The next example is an F♯ diminished arpeggio with extensions from the F♯ Locrian mode, the second mode of the E minor scale. The structure of the Locrian mode is:

F♯ - G - A - B - C - D - E - F♯

R - ♭2 - ♭3 - 4 - ♭5 - ♭6 - ♭7 - 8/Oct.

The extensions Rusty will be using in this example are the minor sixth D at the 22nd fret of the 1st string and the minor second G on the first string 15th fret.

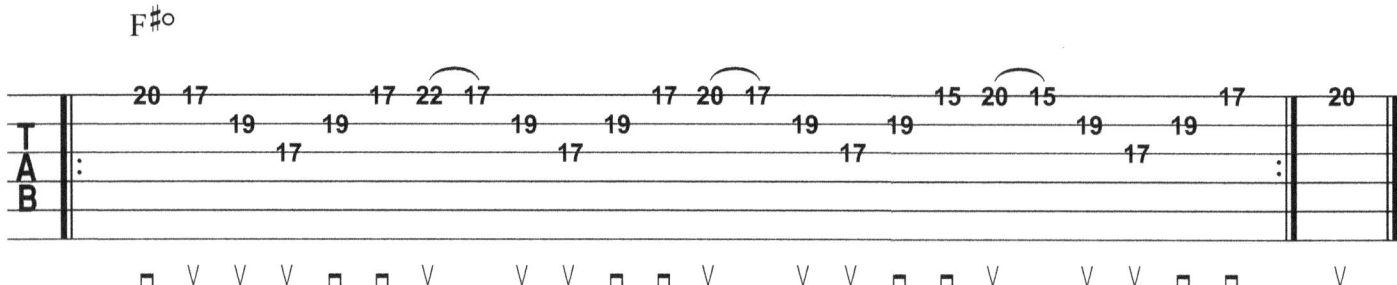

The final example is another C major arpeggio. This time however, Rusty will use the augmented 4th degree F# on the 1st string at the 4th fret as well as the sixth degree A extension again.

Chapter 6:
Fifth String Root Sevenths

"G" Major 7th Arpeggios
In this chapter Rusty will be covering fifth string root seventh arpeggios and some useful alterations you can add to enhance them. To begin this section Rusty starts off with G major seventh arpeggios. In Chapter 2 we discussed that the major arpeggio has three intervals; root - major third - and perfect fifth. The major seventh arpeggio uses the same intervals but also adds in the seventh degree of the scale. So in the context of this lesson the seventh degree of the G major seventh arpeggio is F#. Before we begin playing lets look into where we get this from:

G - A - B - C - D - E - F# - G

R - 2 - 3 - 4 - 5 - 6 - 7 - 8/Oct.

By looking at the previous diagram, you can see that the root is G, the major third is B, the perfect fifth is D and the major seventh degree is F#. When we use just the root, third and fifth it is called three-part harmony, when we include the seventh it becomes four-part harmony. Again if you find any of the theory background to this program confusing, you should pick up a copy of the Rock House Modes Demystified book to clear up any of your questions with the material. A clear understanding of everything being discussed is the surest way to be able to apply the material in your playing.

The first example is a stock root fifth G major seventh arpeggio that begins on the 5th string 10th fret and ascends to the major seventh on the 1st string 14th fret. The picking in this example will be: up - down - down - down - down - down - up (pull-off), up - up - up - up - down.

Notes: G - B - D - F#   Intervals: 1 3 5 7

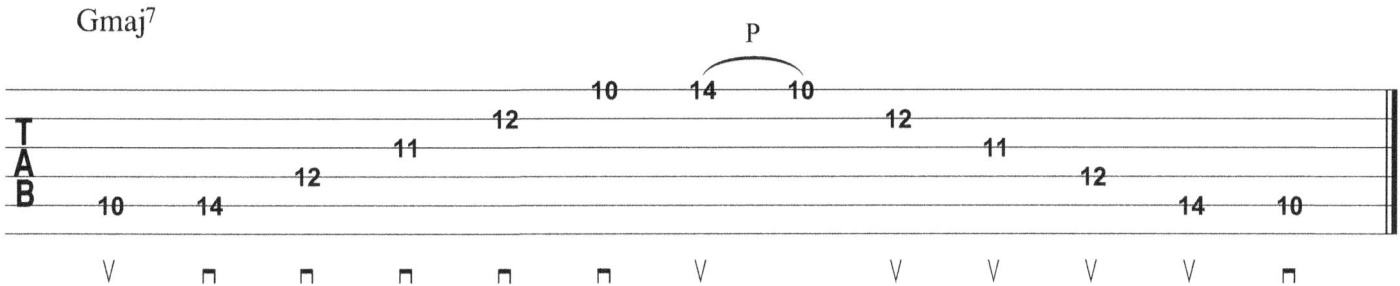

In the next example Rusty takes the previous arpeggio and adds a few alterations for added tonal coloring. First off, Rusty adds in the upper G octave at the 15th fret of the high E string. He plays this added note by using legato on the first string. He ascends the arpeggio as he did in the last example, but now he hammers on then pulls off from the high G note on the 1st string 15th fret. From here he descends as he did in the last example, however, once he reaches the G note on the 5th string 10th fret, he slides down a half step (one fret) to the major seventh F# on the 9th fret and then finally slides back into the root note G at the 10th fret.

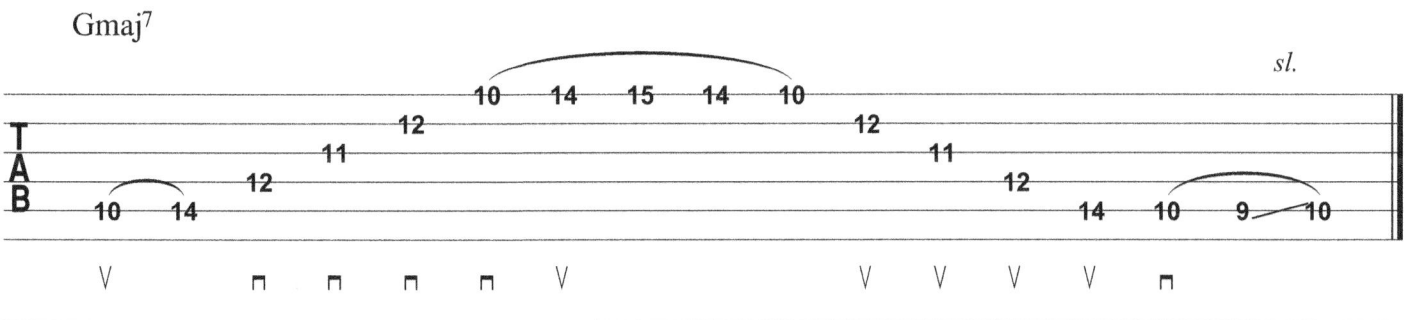

Rusty's Advice!

A lot of times when guitar players are learning to sweep, they think that their difficulties with the technique are stemming from their picking hand, when most of the time it is actually the fretting hand that is the problem. When learning to sweep, a lot of guitar players find that their right and left hands are not syncing up. So Rusty's advice; play the arpeggios without any bars in them all legato.

Take the index finger of your picking hand, reach over onto the neck of your guitar behind your fretting hand and mute all of the strings keeping any string noise to a minimum. Once your picking hand is muting the strings, play the arpeggio using only the strength of your fingers in a legato fashion without any picking what-so-ever.

Example 3 incorporates a pivot on the first string between the F# and at the 14th and 15th frets of the high E string just as we did in the melodic arpeggios lesson in the previous chapter. This is combined with the three to five string sweep arpeggio concept we covered in chapter 4. To finish the arpeggio sequence up Rusty opts for the major seventh for the target note to end on giving a more melodic sound.
In **example 4**, we are going to combine two different three-string shapes together. What

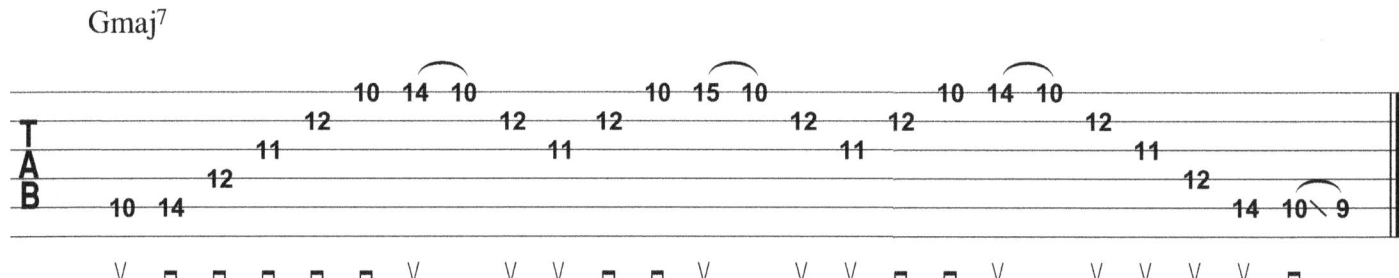

makes this example unique is that when you combine two different shapes (one for the ascend and one for the descend) is that you will be playing in a sweeping fashion without any legato (hammer-ons and pull-offs). The picking for this example will be: down - down - down - up - up - up.
The final G major seventh example is going to expand on the last example. The altera-

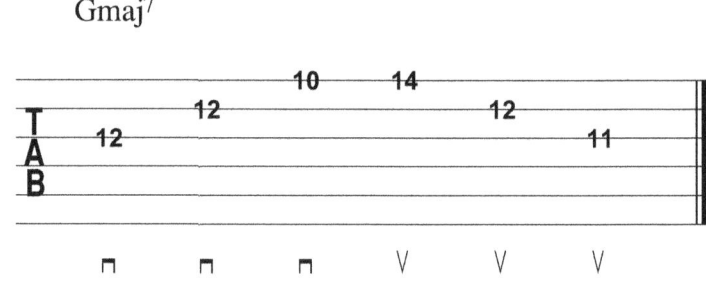

tion in the example will be on the second descend. The F# and G notes will alternate each time you descend the arpeggio.

"A" Minor 7th Arpeggios

In this section Rusty covers a series of A minor seventh arpeggios. In chapter 1 we discussed that the minor arpeggio has three intervals; root - minor third - and perfect fifth. The major seventh arpeggio uses the same intervals but also adds in the minor seventh degree of the scale. So in the context of this lesson the seventh degree of the A minor seventh arpeggio is G. Before we begin playing lets look into where we get this: By looking at the previous diagram, you can see that the root is A, the minor third is C,

A - B - C - D - E - F - G - A
R - 2 - ♭3 - 4 - 5 - ♭6 - ♭7 - 8/Oct.

the perfect fifth is E and the minor seventh degree is G. Just as we said in the major seventh arpeggio section when we use just the root, minor third and fifth it is called three-part harmony, when we include the minor seventh, this is also is considered four-part harmony because of the usage of four different chord tones.

The examples in this section are going to build from the basic arpeggio and add in various alterations just as we did with the G major seventh arpeggios previously. Lets begin with the first example; this is an A minor seventh, root fifth arpeggio, which begins on the root note A, on the 12th fret of the 5th string:
Example 2 adds alterations at the beginning, middle and ending. In this example Rusty

Notes: A - C - E - G   Intervals: 1 ♭3 5 ♭7

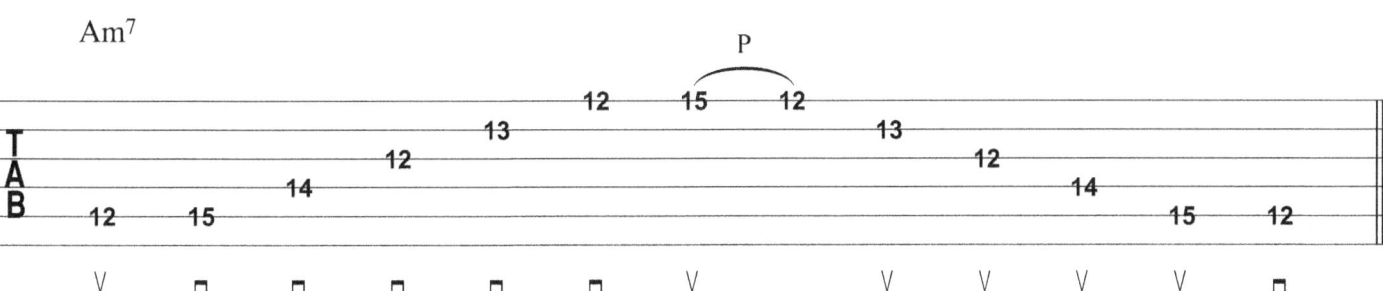

begins by using a series of hammer-ons to begin. He begins on the minor 7th G at the 10th fret with an up-stroke, then he hammers on the root note A and then the minor third C on the 5th string before ascending the arpeggio. From here Rusty plays up the arpeggio as he did in example 1, however the next alteration comes in on the 1st string. This time Rusty adds in the upper octave A note on the 1st string 17th fret by hammering onto the A note from the G note on the 15th fret, and then he pulls back off to the G note before beginning the sweep-picked descend of the arpeggio. The last alteration is just the reversal of the three note legato in the beginning. Rusty plays the C note at the 15th fret of the 5th string then pulls off to the root note A and lastly one more pull-off from the A to the minor seventh G at the 10th fret.
The next example incorporates a pivot on the first string between the G and the A notes

Am⁷

at the 15th and 17th frets of the high E string. Just as in Example 3 of the major seventh arpeggios section, the pivot is combined with the three to five string sweep arpeggio concept.

Example 4 is a full sweeping example combining two different three-string shapes

Amin⁷

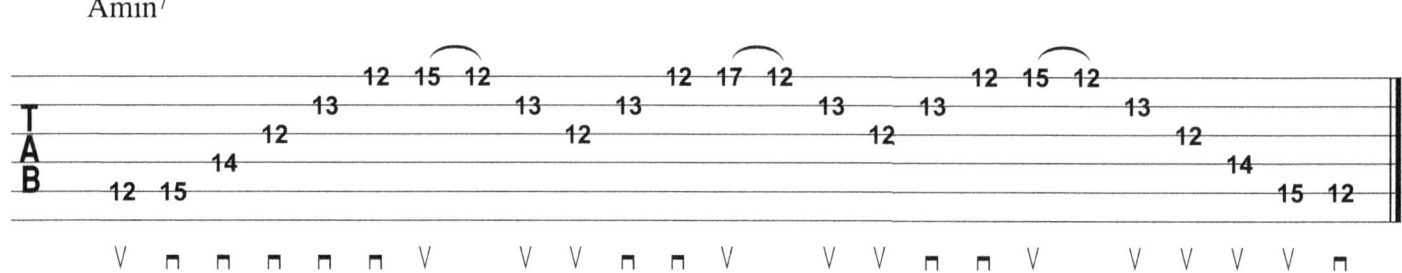

on the first three strings. Rusty ascends A - C - E (the A minor triad) and then descends G - C - G the minor seventh and the minor third.

Am⁷

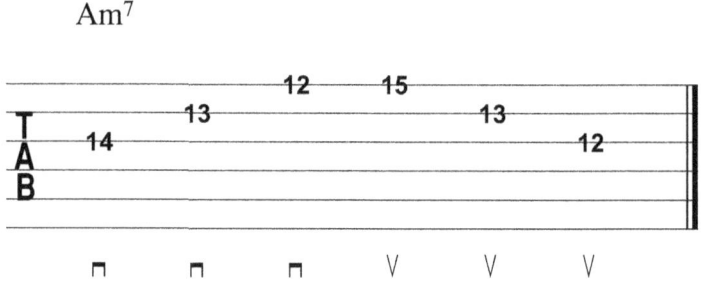

In the final minor seventh example you are still playing the three note sweeping arpeggio as before, but, it incorporates a pivot between the minor 7th G and the root note A on the 1st string.

"A" Dominant 7th Arpeggios

Am⁷

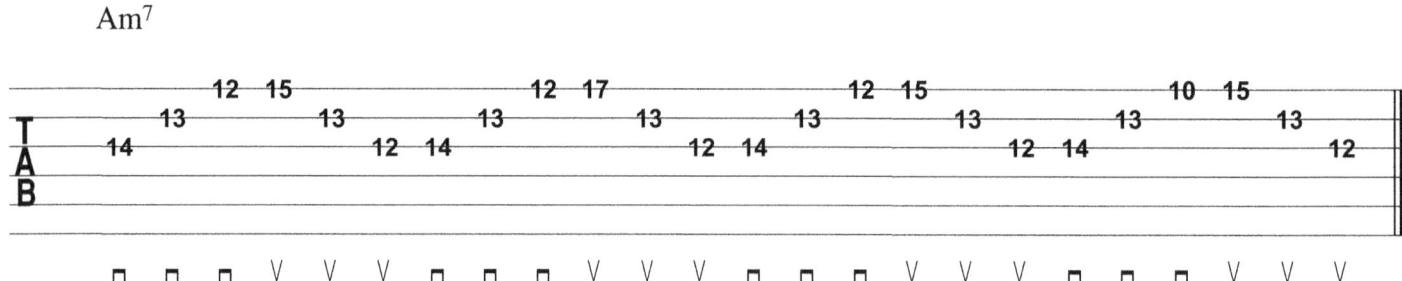

In this section Rusty continues on the four-part harmony path by diving into the dominant seventh arpeggios. Dominant arpeggios are derived from the fifth mode of the major scale Mixolydian. So let's begin by looking at the A Mixolydian mode (fifth mode of D major) and see where the A dominant seventh arpeggios originate:

As you can see the Mixolydian mode contains the A major triad A - C# - E however the

A - B - C# - D - E - F# - G - A
R - 2 - 3 - 4 - 5 - 6 - ♭7 - 8/Oct.

flatted 7th G creates the "funky" or "bluesy" sound associated with the dominant family. The reason is that the major third and minor seventh intervals create tension because they are a diminished fifth interval apart. These are things you will really want to pay attention to. By seeing this you will see connections to other arpeggio shapes to superimpose as you gain great knowledge of the arpeggios and theory. For example, once you get these dominant arpeggios together, try taking the diminished arpeggios we covered earlier and play them starting on C# over an A dominant seventh chord to hear some really hip sounds, then try to link C# diminished and a minor seventh arpeggios together. The idea is to always look within the notes to see what else is available to you that you already know so you can expand your tonal color range while improvising.

Lets take a look at **Example 1** and get the root fifth A dominant seventh arpeggio under your fingers then we will move onto the extended alterations as we have previously:
Example 2 adds in the minor seventh extensions on the 5th and 1st strings as in the

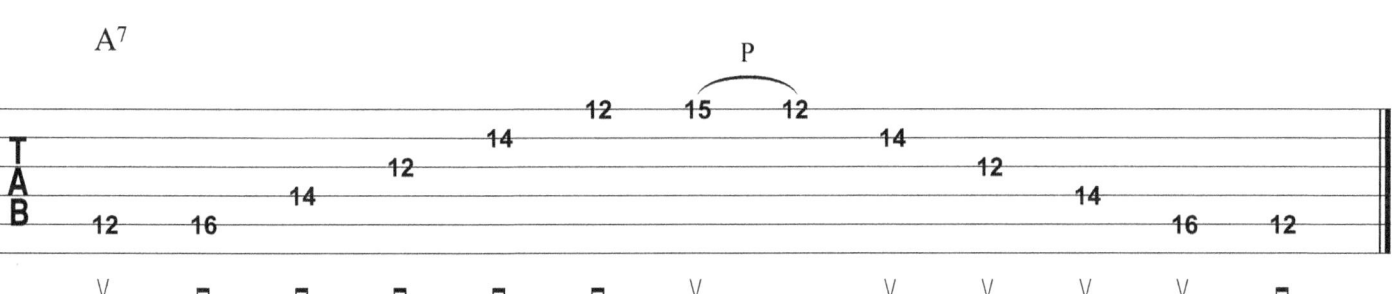

previous examples. Make sure your picking is accurate and that the notes when played with legato sound clearly.
Example 3 incorporates the three to five string sweep concept and a pivot between the

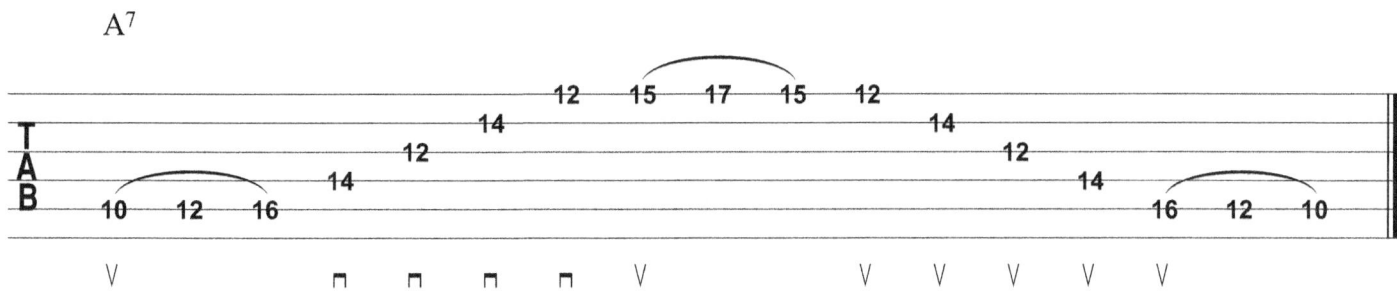

minor seventh G and root A notes on the 1st string:
Example 4 is a another three-string full sweeping example combining two different shapes.

33

A⁷

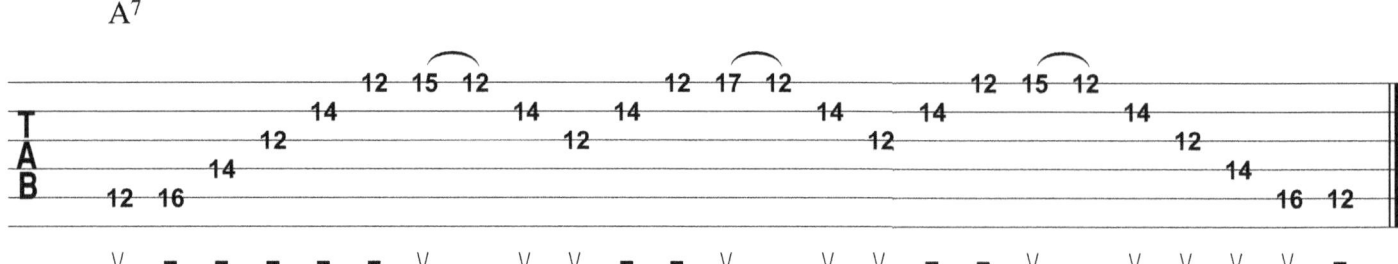

Rusty ascends A - C♯ - E (the A major triad) and then descends G - C♯ - G the minor seventh and the major third.

A⁷

The last example, just as in the two previous seventh arpeggio sections is a three-string sweeping pattern that combines example 4 and a pivot between the root and minor seventh scale tones on the 1st string.

A⁷

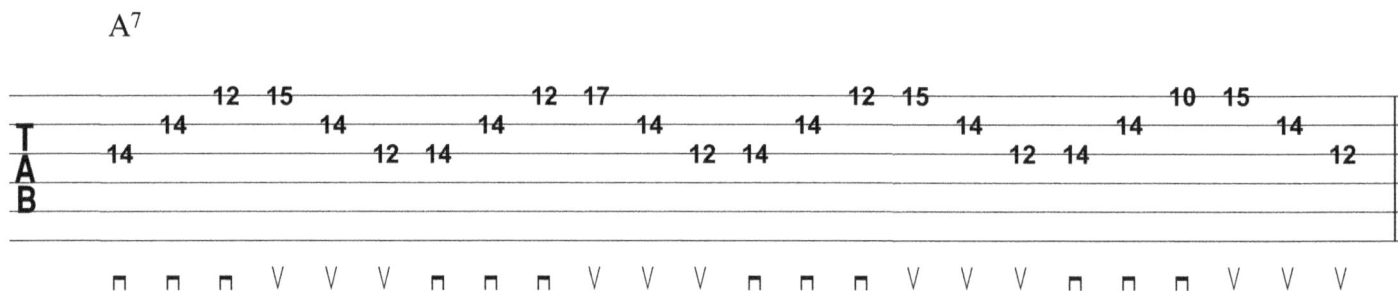

Next up is the minor seventh flat five arpeggios built from F♯. These arpeggios combine the diminished triad; root - minor third - diminished fifth and the minor seventh intervals of the Locrian mode (seventh mode of the major scale). In this case F♯ Locrian is derived from the G major scales seventh degree so it shares the exact same notes, however the root note is shifted to F♯. Lets look at the arpeggios pedigree for a deeper understanding:

F♯ - G - A - B - C - D - E - F♯
R - ♭2 - ♭3 - 4 - ♭5 - ♭6 - ♭7 - 8/Oct.

So as you can see here the root F♯, minor third G, diminished fifth C and minor seventh E all combine to make the "minor seven flat five" four-part harmony used within these arpeggios.

So now that we have covered the basics of the arpeggios origin, lets dive into the arpeggios and alterations. Example 1 is the root position 5th string F#m7b5 arpeggio we will be building from:

Notes: F# - A - C - E   Intervals: 1 b3 b5 b7

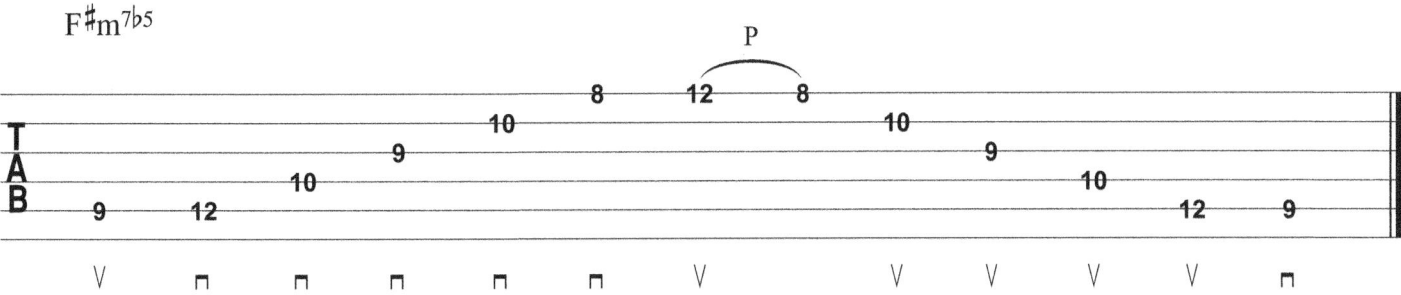

The second example will add the legato rolls on the 5th and 1st strings by adding in the minor seventh just as we have done in the previous sections of this chapter:

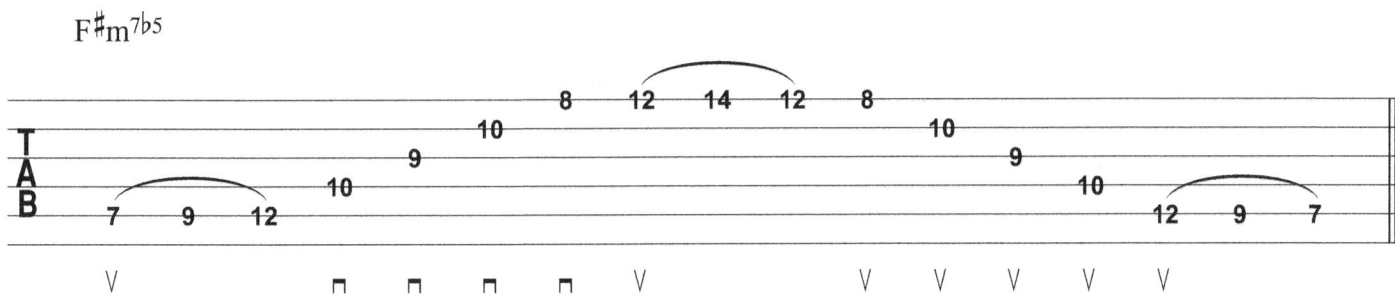

Example 3 is a five and three string arpeggio sequence combined with alternating notes on the 1st string. The sequence will alternate between E and F# giving a melodic feel.

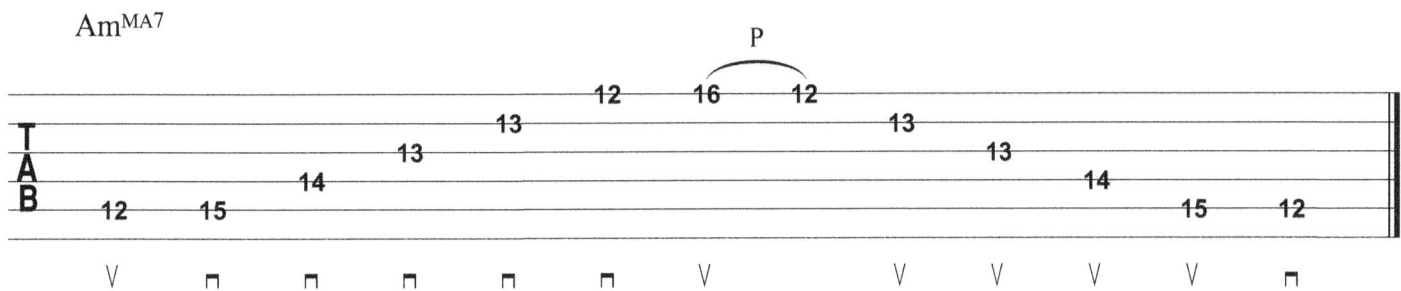

Example 4 is two three string shapes that use the ascend sweep and descend sweep picking just as with the previous seventh arpeggios.

35

Example 5 uses the same three string sequence as we just used in Example 4, however, he adds in the extensions of F♯ (14th fret) and B (7th fret) on the 1st string.

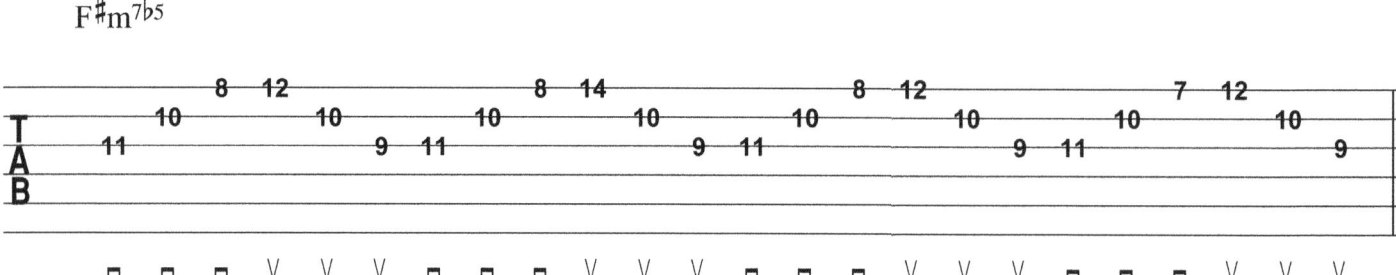

Chapter 7:
Additional Seventh Arpeggio Concepts

The next five examples will expand on the seventh arpeggio concepts we just looked at in the previous lessons. Examples 1 and 2 will use a combination of basic triads alternating with their corresponding seventh shapes, and examples 3, 4 and 5 will look at arpeggios derived from the Harmonic and Melodic minor scales.

Example 1 is based on A minor and will alternate between an A minor arpeggio and an A minor seventh arpeggio. The trick part of this sequence is the string skipping from the first string to the 3rd string right after the first pull off in the sequence. Follow the picking pattern closely and work slowly on this sequence while getting it under your fingers.

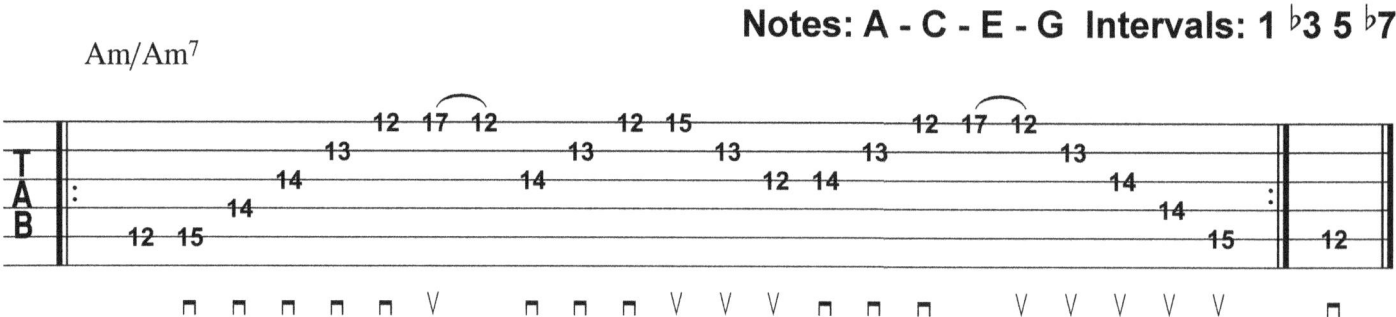

Example 2 combines the A Major and A Major Seventh arpeggios using the same pattern as in example 1.

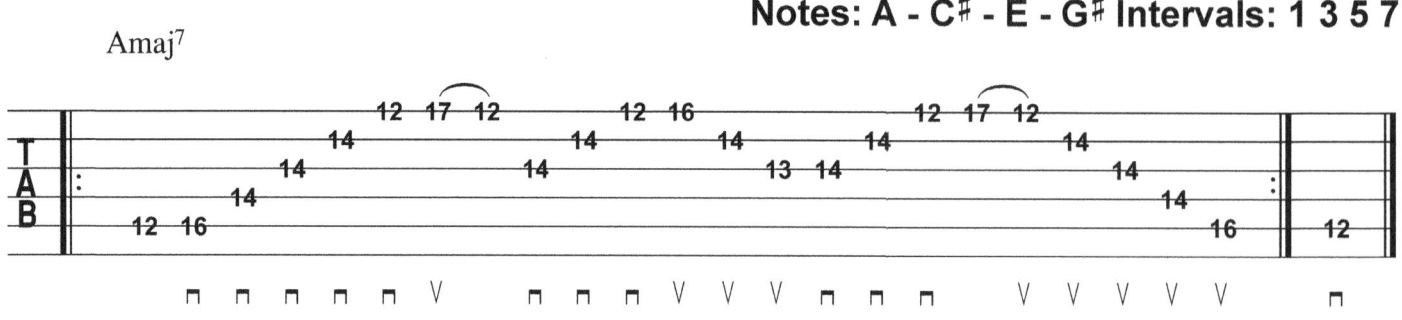

Example 3 is an A minor Major Seven arpeggio. The A minor Major Seven chord is the 1 chord in A Harmonic minor.

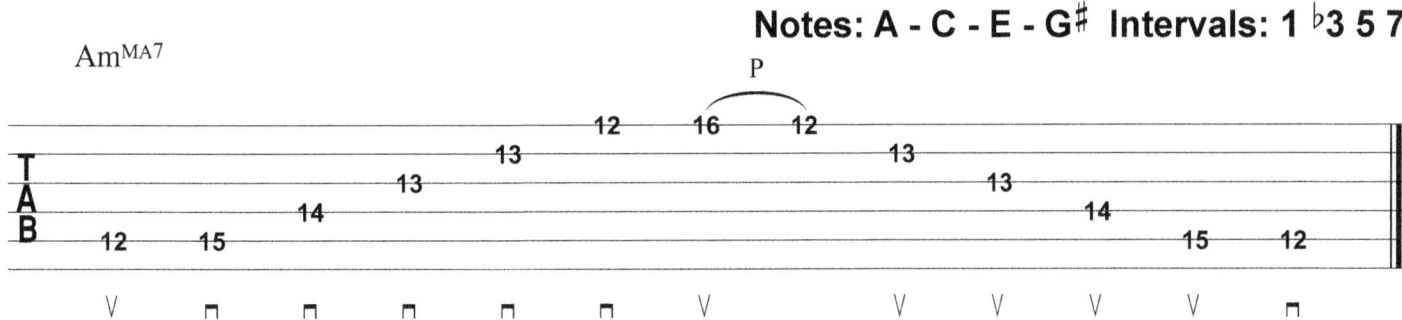

Examples 4 and 5 are A Minor Seven sharp five sequences. The Am7#5 is the three chord of the Harmonic minor and Melodic minor scales.

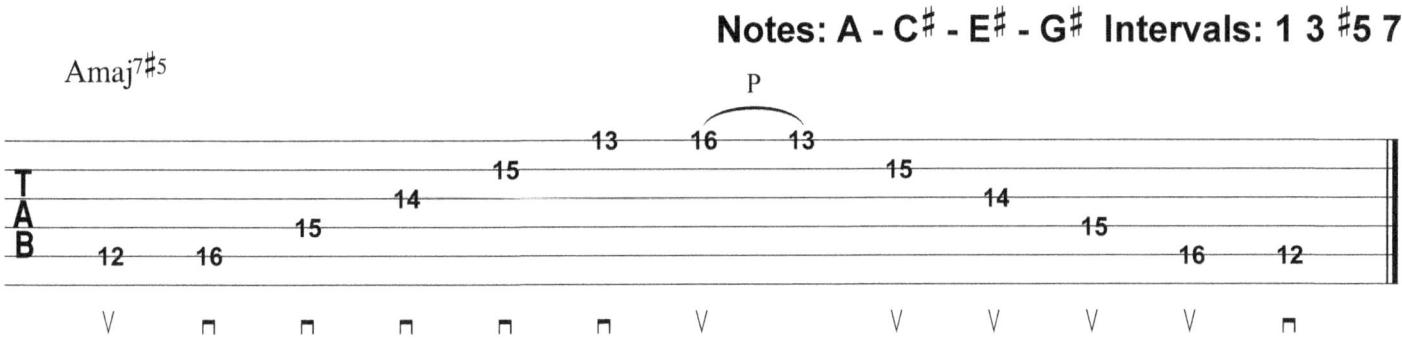

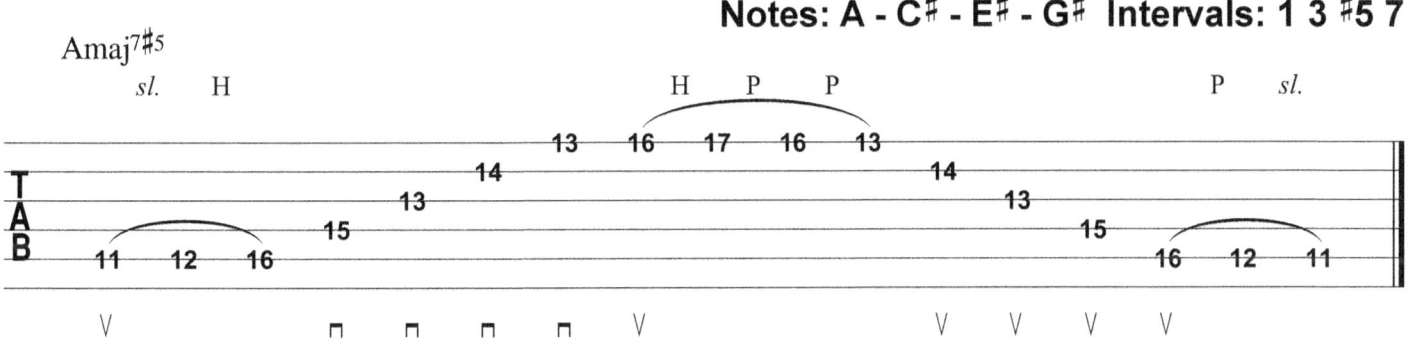

Chapter 8: Combining Arpeggios with Chromatic Passing Tones

In this section we are going to look at how to combine two diatonic arpeggios together by using chromatic passing tones. These ideas were inspired by listening to Classical composers such as Chopan.

Example 1 combines the arpeggios A minor and D minor. The common tone that ties the two shapes together is the A note on the 5th string. If you are approaching this in the key of A minor, the D minor arpeggio is the four chord of A minor and the A note is the 5th degree of the D minor chord. If you were to approach this from the key of D minor, the A minor chord is the five chord, so you can use this in either key, the A note is shared by both arpeggios and makes them transition smoothly together. The "Classical" sound comes from the chromatic notes on the 1st string where the actual shift between the arpeggios occurs. The 5th degree of the A minor triad "E" shifts to the minor third degree "F" of D minor after the chromatic passage of A, G♯ and G on the 1st string.

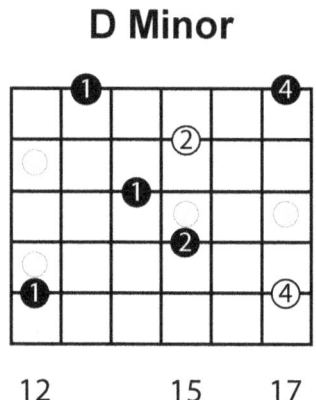

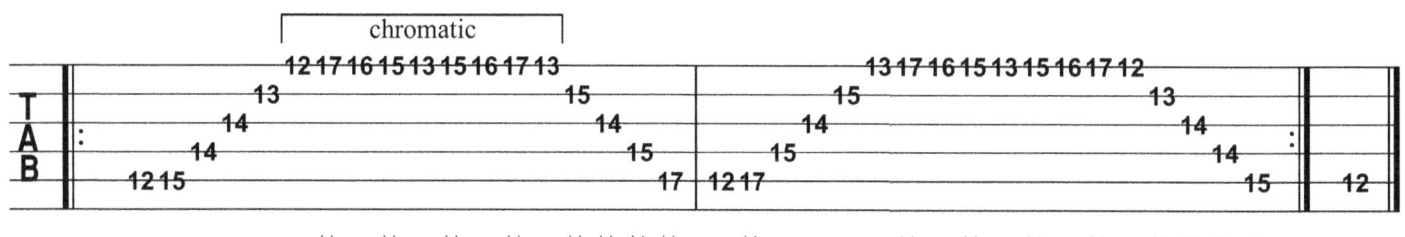

Example 2 uses the exact same concept but combines together an A Major and D Major arpeggio. The shift in this sequence occurs in the same place on the 1st string, however, the 5th degree of A Major "E" on the 1st string shifts to the Major third F♯ of the D Major arpeggio on the 14th fret.

Notes: A - C♯ - E Intervals: 1 3 5   Notes: D - F♯ - A Intervals: 1 3 5

A Major

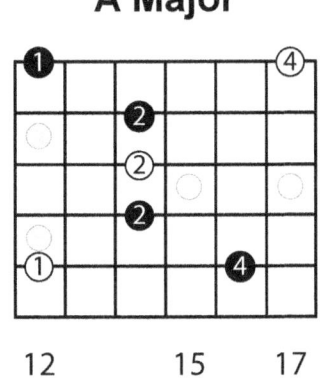

D Major

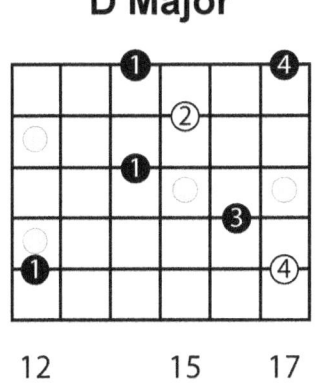

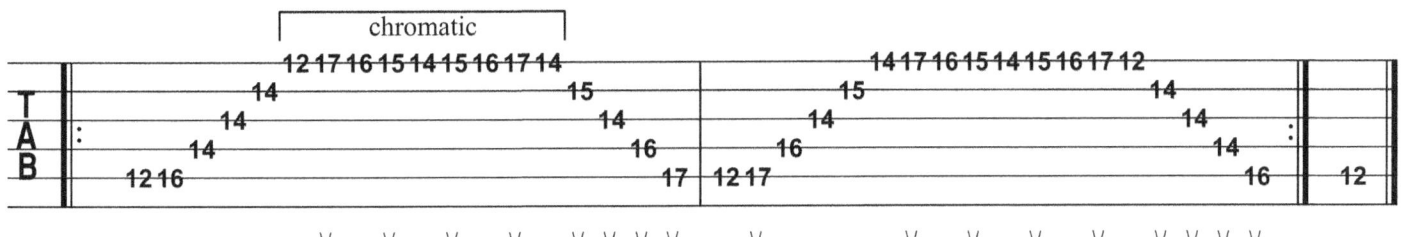

Program 2

Chapter 9: Diatonic 11th Arpeggios in the Key of "G" Major

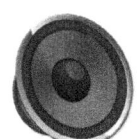

The group of arpeggios we are going to look at are 11th arpeggios that are diatonic to the key of "G" major. These arpeggios are diatonic because they only use the notes of the G Major scale G, A, B, C, D, E and F♯. Eleventh arpeggios are created by playing the Root, Third, Fifth, Seventh, Ninth and Eleventh degrees of the scale. It may take your ear some adjustment to get used to the sound of these extended harmony arpeggios especially if you are only used to the sounds of the basic triads.

Example 1 is G Major 11 and uses the Root, Major Third, Perfect Fifth, Major Seventh, Major Ninth and Perfect Eleventh of the G Major Scale (G, B, D, F♯, A and C).

Gmaj¹¹ — **Notes: G - B - D - F# - A - C Intervals: 1 3 5 7 9 11**

Example 2 is a Am11 arpeggio derived form the second mode of the G Major Scale starting on the second note of the scale A, the A Dorian mode. The intervals used are the Root, minor Third, Perfect Fifth, minor Seventh, Major Ninth and Perfect Eleventh degrees (A, C, E, G, B and D).

Am¹¹ — **Notes: A - C - E - G - B - D Intervals: 1 ♭3 5 ♭7 9 11**

Example 3 is a Bm11♭9 arpeggio derived form the third mode of the G Major Scale starting on the third note of the scale B, the B Phrygian mode. The intervals used are the Root, minor Third, Perfect Fifth, minor Seventh, minor Ninth and Perfect Eleventh degrees (B, D, F#, A, C and E).

Bm¹¹♭⁹ — **Notes: B - D - F# - A - C - E Intervals: 1 ♭3 5 ♭7 ♭9 11**

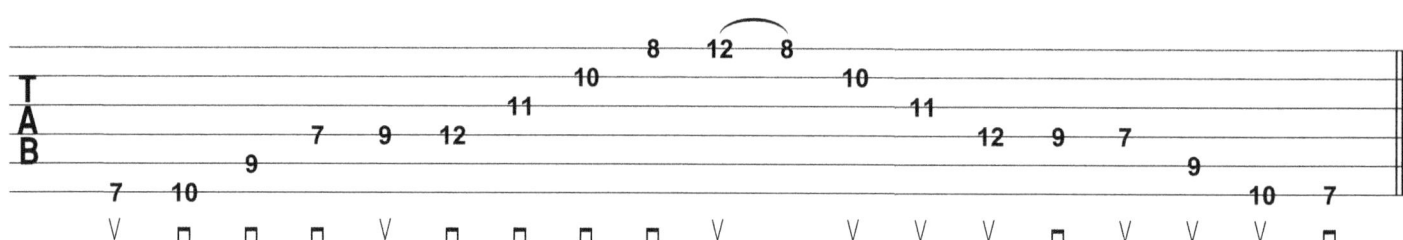

Example 4 is a C Major 9# 11 arpeggio derived from the fourth mode of the G Major Scale C Lydian starting on the fourth note of the G Major scale C. The intervals used are the Root, Major Third, Perfect Fifth, Major Seventh, Major Ninth and Augmented Eleventh degrees (C, E, G, B, D and F#).

Cmaj9#11   **Notes: C - E - G - B - D - F# Intervals: 1 3 5 7 9 #11**

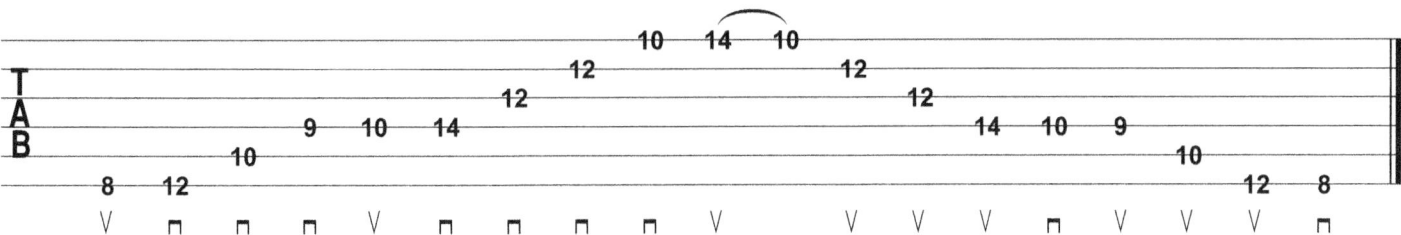

Example 5 is a D11 arpeggio derived form the fifth mode of the G Major Scale D Mixolydian starting on the fifth note of the G Major scale D. The intervals used are the Root, Major Third, Perfect Fifth, minor Seventh, Major Ninth and Perfect Eleventh degrees (D, F#, A, C, E and G).

D11   **Notes: D - F# - A - C - E - G Intervals: 1 3 5 b7 9 11**

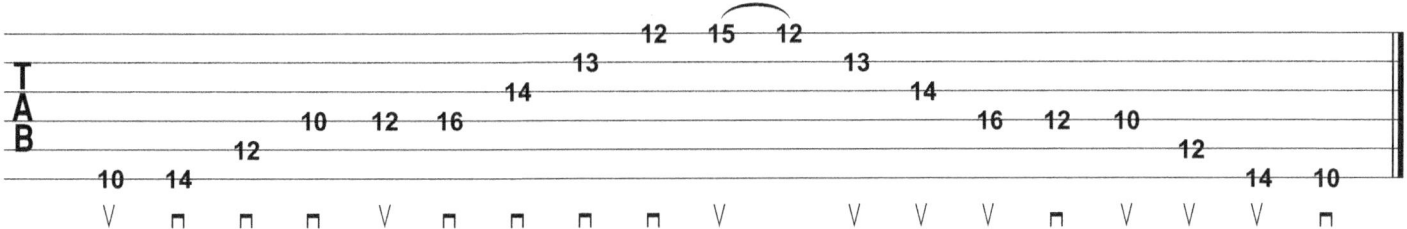

Example 6 is an Em11 arpeggio derived form the sixth mode of the G Major Scale E Aeolian starting on the sixth note of the G Major scale E. The intervals used are the Root, minor Third, Perfect Fifth, minor Seventh, Major Ninth and Perfect Eleventh degrees (E, G, B, D, F# and A).

Em11   **Notes: E - G - B - D - F# - A Intervals: 1 b3 5 b7 9 11**

Example 7 is an F#m7b5b911 arpeggio derived form the seventh mode of the G Major Scale F# Locrian starting on the seventh note of the G Major scale F#. The intervals used are the Root, minor Third, diminished Fifth, minor Seventh, minor Ninth and Perfect Eleventh degrees (F#, A, C, E, G and B).

F#m7b5b911   **Notes: F# - A - C - E - G - B Intervals: 1 b3 b5 b7 b9 11**

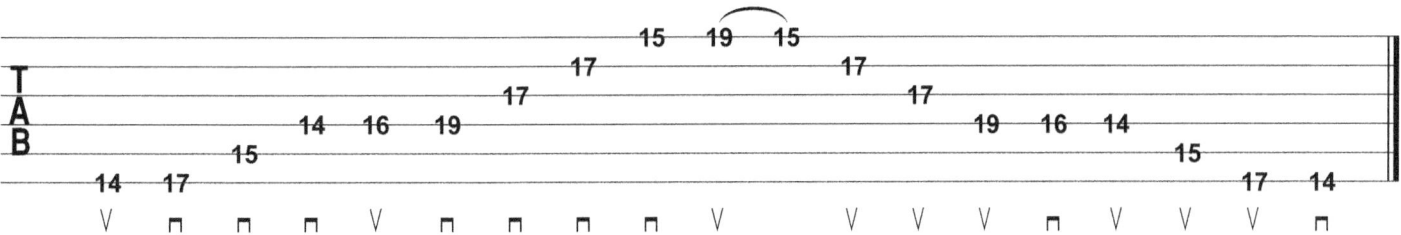

Chapter 10: Diatonic 13th Arpeggios in the Key of "G" Major

The next step to building the extended arpeggios is to add the 13th to the 11th arpeggios we just covered. So the new intervallic make up these arpeggios will be Root, Second, Third, Fifth, Seventh, Ninth, Eleventh and Thirteenth. Just as in the last section, all of these Arpeggios will be diatonic to the key of G Major and relative to the modes of the G Major scale. This means that each modes interval will vary depending on the mode just as they did with the 11th arpeggios we just covered.

Example 1 is a Gmaj13 arpeggio and has the intervals Root, Major Third, Perfect Fifth, Major Seventh, Major Ninth, Perfect Eleventh and Major Thirteenth (G, B, D, F#, A, C and E). Notice that all of the notes of the scale are used in the arpeggio as well as all of the others in this section.

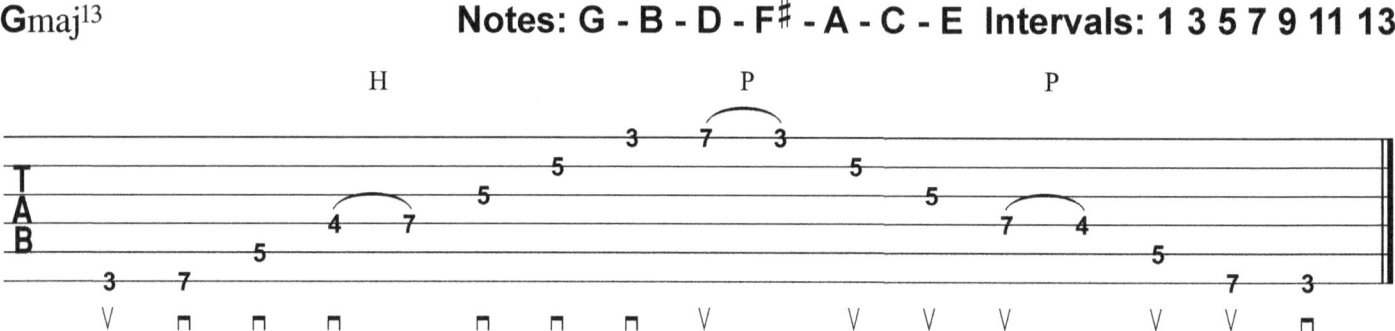

Example 2 is an Amin13 arpeggio derived form the second mode of the G Major Scale A Dorian starting on the second note of the G Major scale A. The intervals used are the Root, minor Third, Perfect Fifth, minor Seventh, Major Ninth, Perfect Eleventh and Major Thirteenth degrees (A, C, E, G, B, D and F#).

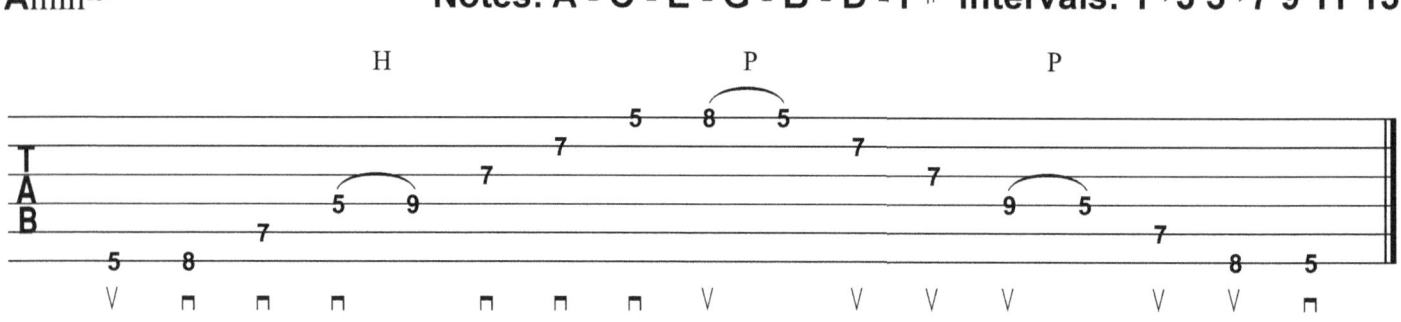

Example 3 is a Bmin♭13♭9 arpeggio derived form the third mode of the G Major Scale B Phrygian starting on the third note of the G Major scale B. The intervals used are the Root, minor Third, Perfect Fifth, minor Seventh, minor Ninth, Perfect Eleventh and minor Thirteenth degrees (B, D, F♯, A, C, E and G).

Bmin♭13♭9 **Notes: B - D - F♯ - A - C - E - G Intervals: 1 ♭3 5 ♭7 ♭9 11 ♭13**

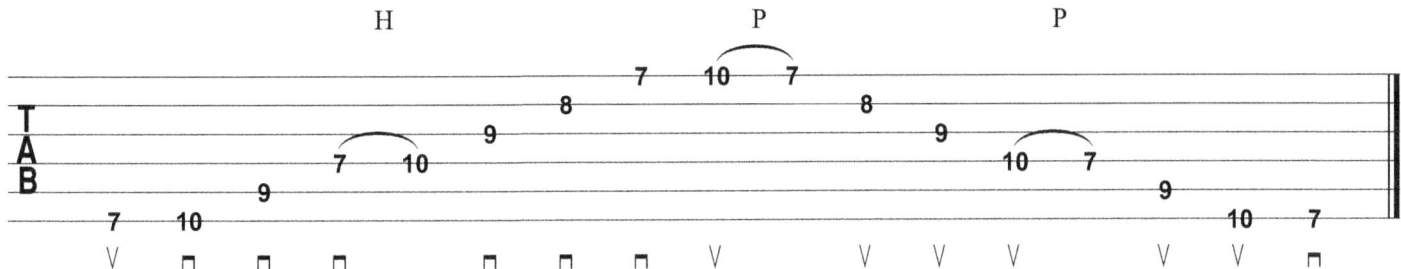

Example 4 is a Cmaj13♯11 arpeggio derived form the fourth mode of the G Major Scale C Lydian starting on the fourth note of the G Major scale C. The intervals used are the Root, Major Third, Perfect Fifth, Major Seventh, Major Ninth, Augmented Eleventh and Major Thirteenth degrees (C, E, G, B, D, F♯ and A).

Cmaj13♯11 **Notes: C - E - G - B - D - F♯ - A Intervals: 1 3 5 7 9 ♯11 13**

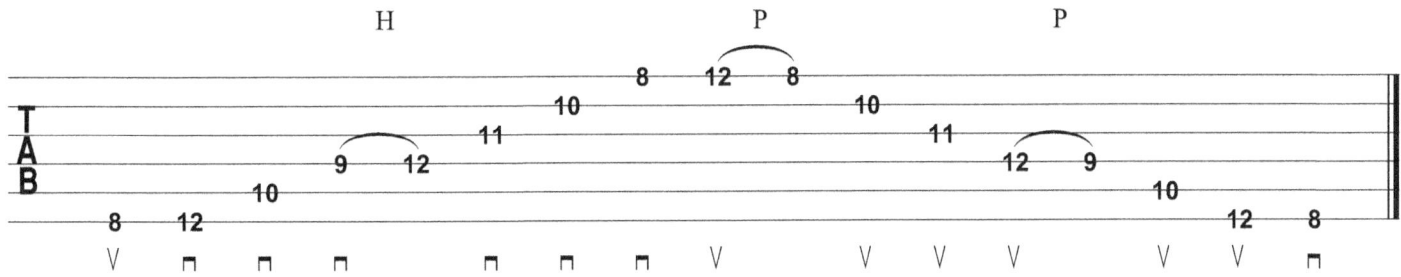

Example 5 is a D13 arpeggio derived form the fifth mode of the G Major Scale D Mixolydian starting on the fifth note of the G Major scale D. The intervals used are the Root, Major Third, Perfect Fifth, minor Seventh, Major Ninth, Perfect Eleventh and Major Thirteenth degrees (D, F♯, A, C, E, G and B).

D13 **Notes: D - F♯ - A - C - E - G - B Intervals: 1 3 5 ♭7 9 11 13**

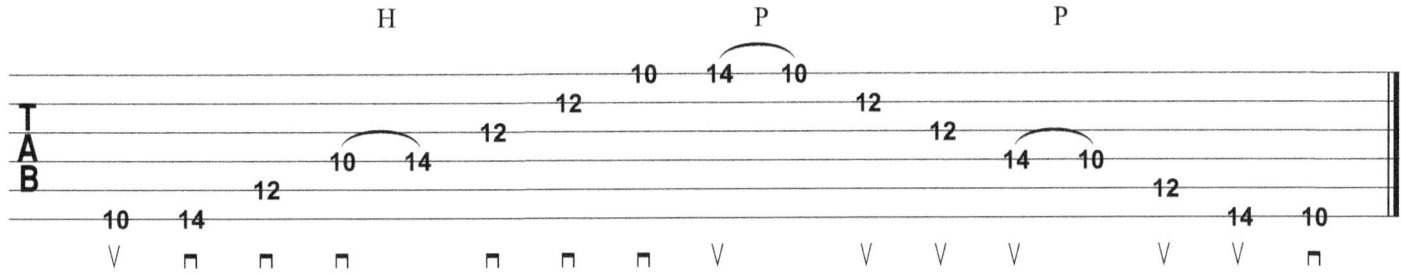

Example 6 is a Emb13 arpeggio derived form the Sixth mode of the G Major Scale E Aeolian starting on the sixth note of the G Major scale E. The intervals used are the Root, minor Third, Perfect Fifth, minor Seventh, Major Ninth, Perfect Eleventh and minor Thirteenth degrees (E, G, B, D, F#, A and C).

Em♭13   Notes: E - G - B - D - F# - A - C   Intervals: 1 ♭3 5 ♭7 9 11 ♭13

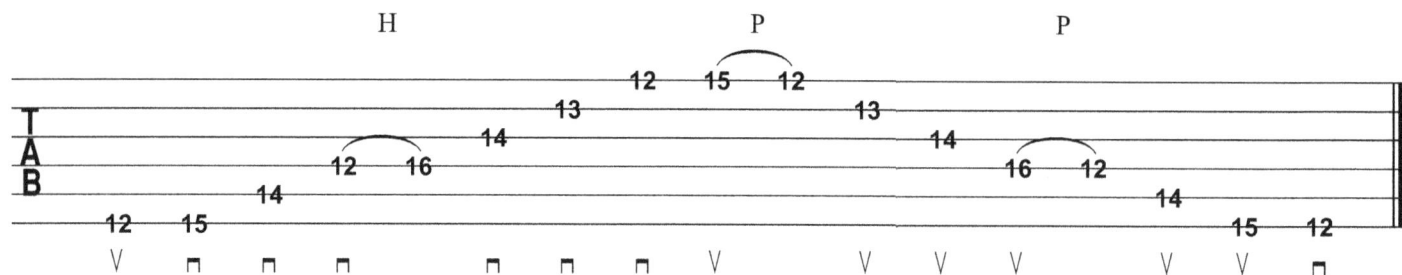

Example 7 is a F#7♭5♭9♭13 arpeggio derived form the Seventh mode of the G Major Scale F# Locrian starting on the seventh note of the G Major scale F#. The intervals used are the Root, minor Third, diminished Fifth, minor Seventh, minor Ninth, Perfect Eleventh and minor Thirteenth degrees (F#, A, C, E, G, B and D).

Fm#7♭5♭9♭13   Notes: F# - A - C - E - G - B - D   Intervals: 1 ♭3 ♭5 ♭7 ♭9 11 ♭13

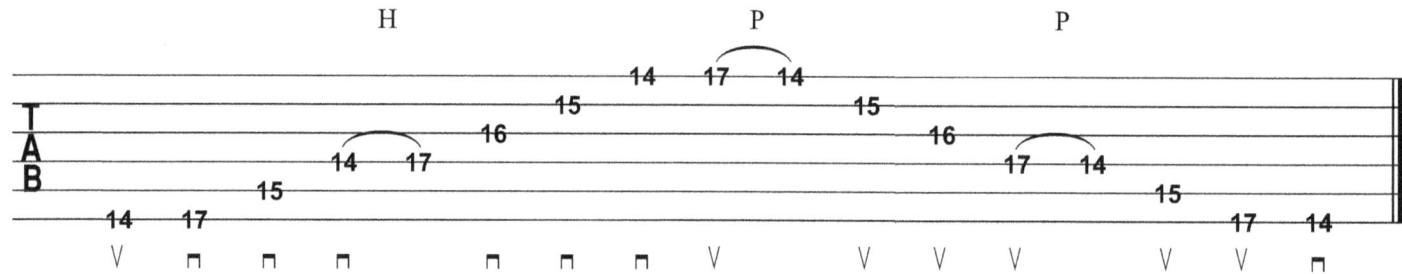

Chapter 11: Extended Diatonic Arpeggios in the Key of "G" Major

In this lesson we are going to dive deeper into the diatonic 13th arpeggios in the key of G Major. However this time we are going to make extended patterns that stretch in a more linear fashion across the neck of your guitar. Jut as with the previous 11th and 13th arpeggios we covered, these will all be diatonic to the G Major Scale and the modes derived from G Major.

Example 1 is a Gmaj13 arpeggio based on the G Major Scale or Ionian mode and spans from the 3rd fret of the 6th string up to the 10th fret of the 1st string.

Gmaj¹³ **Notes: G - B - D - F♯ - A - C - E Intervals: 1 3 5 7 9 11 13**

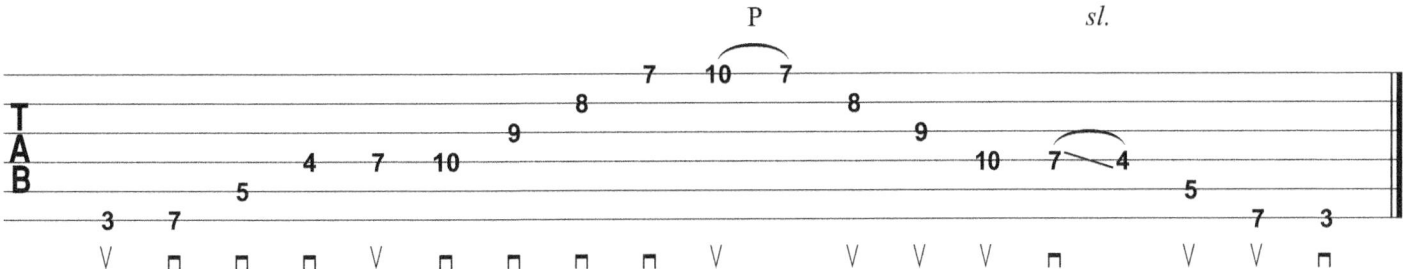

Example 2 is an Am13 arpeggio based on the A Dorian mode and spans from the 5th fret of the 6th string up to the 12th fret of the 1st string.

Am¹³ **Notes: A - C - E - G - B - D - F♯ Intervals: 1 ♭3 5 ♭7 9 11 13**

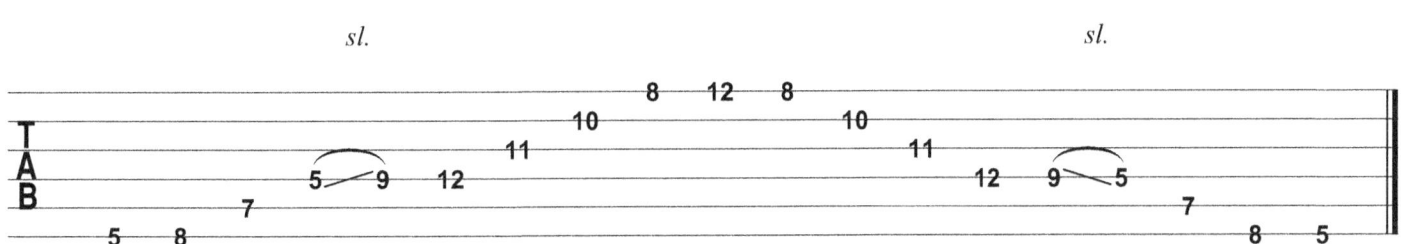

Example 3 is a Bm13♭9 arpeggio based on the B Phrygian mode and spans from the 7th fret of the 6th string up to the 14th fret of the 1st string.

Bm¹³♭⁹ **Notes: B - D - F♯ - A - C - E - G Intervals: 1 ♭3 5 ♭7 ♭9 11 ♭13**

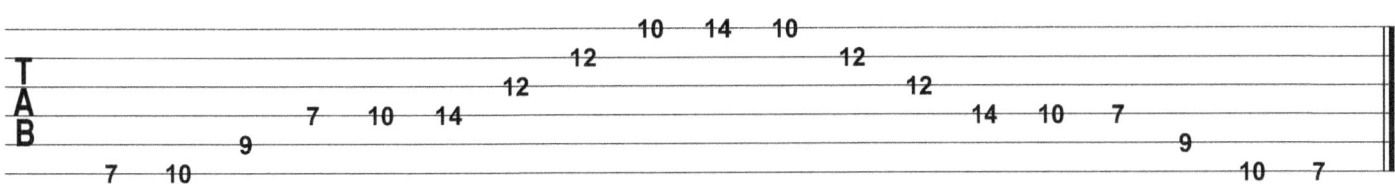

Example 4 is a Cmaj13♯11 arpeggio based on the C Lydian mode and spans from the eighth fret of the sixth string up to the fifteenth fret of the first string.

Cmaj¹³♯¹¹ **Notes: C - E - G - B - D - F♯ - A Intervals: 1 3 5 7 9 ♯11 13**

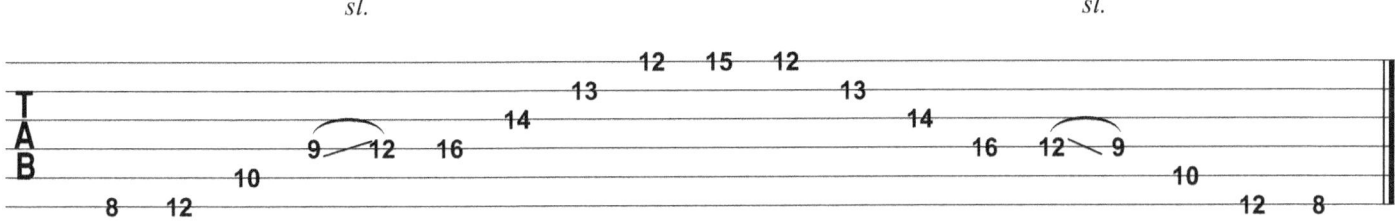

Example 5 is a D13 arpeggio based on the D Mixolydian mode and spans from the 10th fret of the 6th string up to the 17th fret of the 1st string.

D¹³   **Notes: D - F♯ - A - C - E - G - B Intervals: 1 3 5 ♭7 9 11 13**

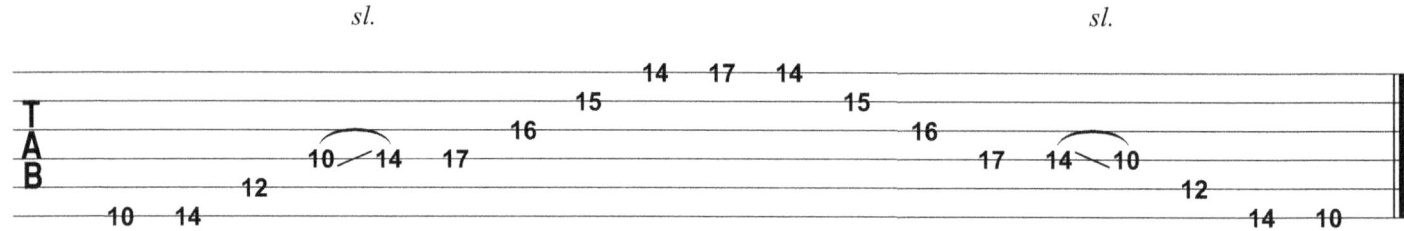

Example 6 is a Em13 arpeggio based on the E Aeolian mode and spans from the 12th fret of the 6th string up to the 19th fret of the 1st string.

Em♭¹³   **Notes: E - G - B - D - F♯ - A - C Intervals: 1 ♭3 5 ♭7 9 11 ♭13**

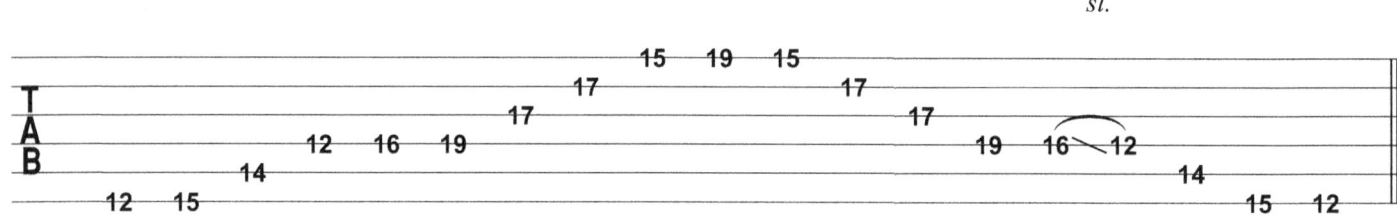

Example 7 is an F♯m♭13♭5♭9 arpeggio based on the F♯ Locrian mode and spans from the 14th fret of the 6th string up to the 12th fret of the 1st string.

F♯m♭¹³♭⁵♭⁹   **Notes: F♯ - A - C - E - G - B - D Intervals: 1 ♭3 ♭5 ♭7 ♭9 11 ♭13**

Chapter 12: Diatonic 13th Arpeggios in the Key of "B" Harmonic Minor

In this lesson we are going to be looking at the extended arpeggios relative to the B Harmonic Minor scale and its derived modes. The first arpeggio we are going to look at is the Bm/maj7b13 arpeggio derived from the Root note of the Harmonic Minor Scale. The notes used are B, D, F#, A#, C#, E and G, the intervals are Root, minor Third, Perfect Fifth, Major Seventh, Major Ninth, Perfect Eleventh and minor 13th degrees.

Bm/maj⁷♭¹³   Notes: B - D - F# - A# - C# - E - G   Intervals: 1 ♭3 5 7 ♭9 11 ♭13

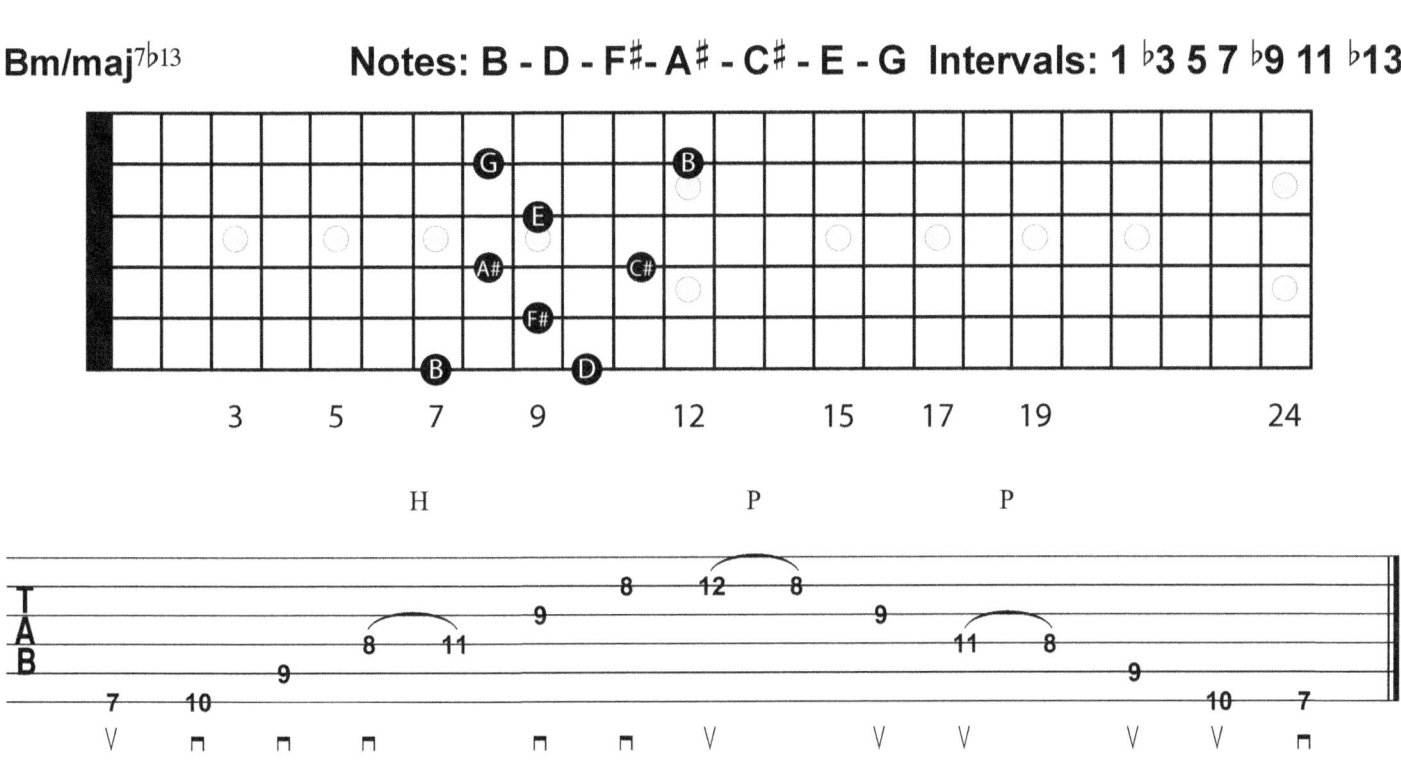

Example 2 is a C#m7b5b913 arpeggio based on the second mode of the Harmonic minor Scale; Locrian #6, and consists of the intervals Root, minor third, diminished fifth, minor seventh, minor ninth, Perfect eleventh and Major thirteenth.

C#m⁷♭⁵♭⁹¹³   Notes: C# - E - G - B - D - F# - A#   Intervals: 1 ♭3 ♭5 ♭7 ♭9 11 ♭13

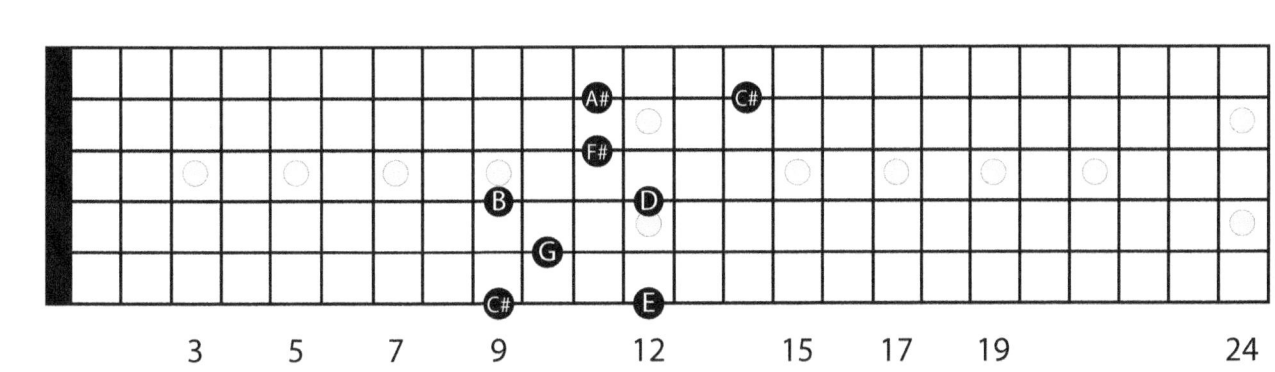

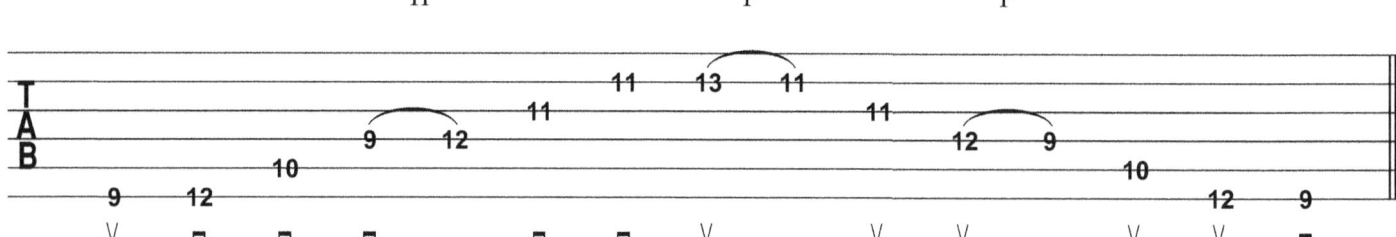

Example 3 is a Dmaj13#5 arpeggio based on the third mode of the Harmonic minor Scale; Ionian Augmented, and consists of the intervals Root, Major third, augmented fifth, Major seventh, Major ninth, Perfect eleventh and Major thirteenth.

Dmaj13#5   Notes: D - F# - A# - C# - E - G - B   Intervals: 1 3 #5 7 9 11 13

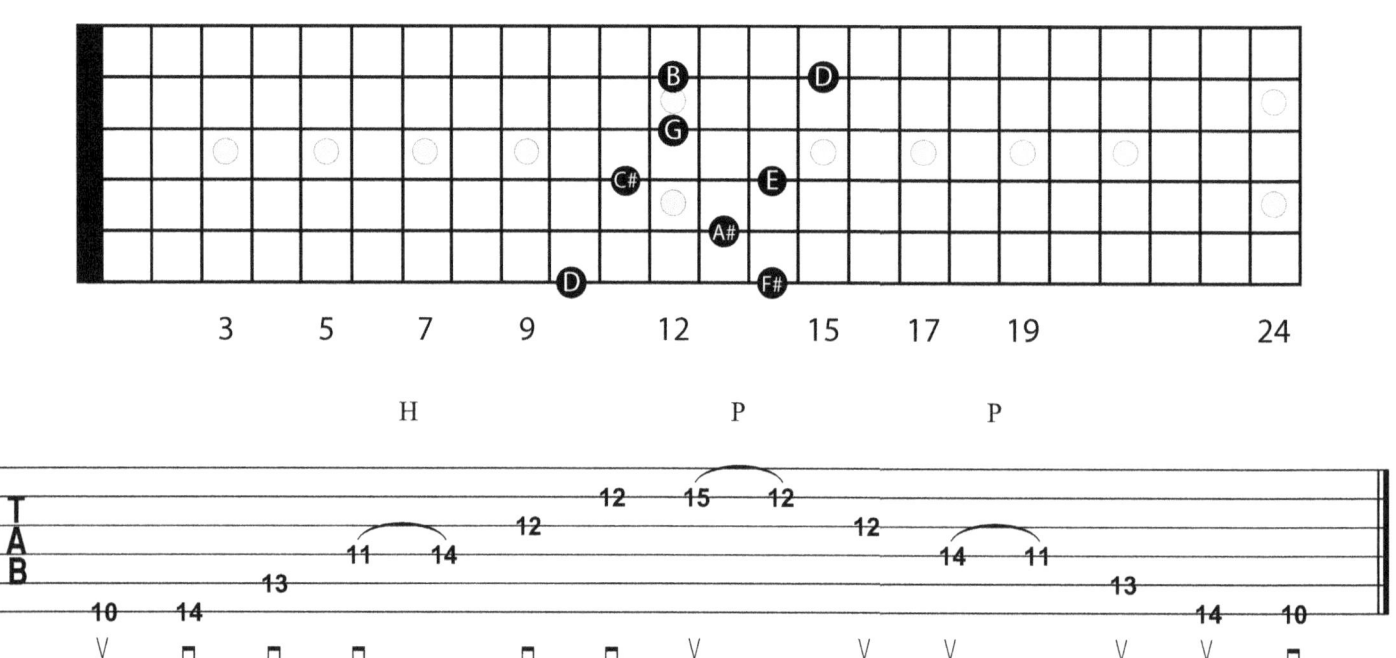

Example 4 is a Em13#11 arpeggio based on the fourth mode of the Harmonic minor Scale; Dorian #4, and consists of the intervals Root, minor third, Perfect fifth, minor seventh, Major ninth, augmented eleventh and Major thirteenth.

Em13#11   Notes: E - G - B - D - F# - A# - C#   Intervals: 1 b3 5 b7 9 #11 13

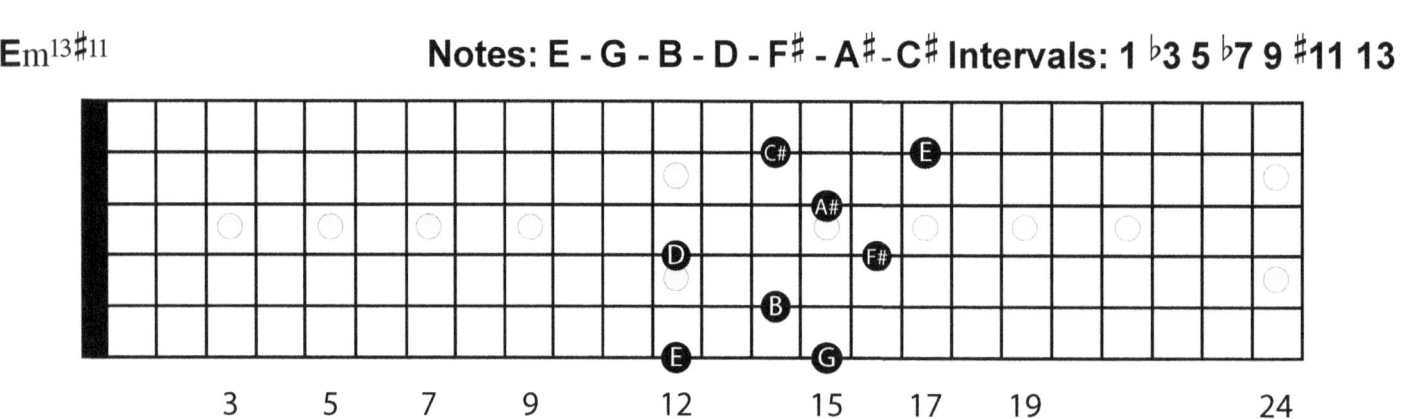

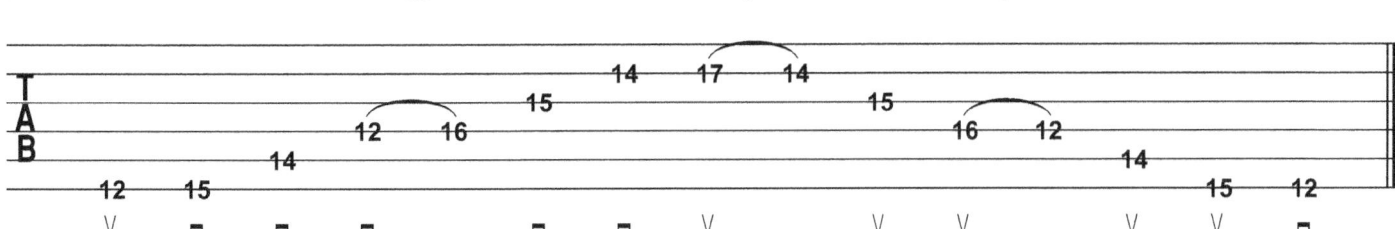

Example 5 is a F#7b9b13 arpeggio based on the fifth mode of the Harmonic minor Scale; Phrygian Major, and consists of the intervals Root, Major third, Perfect fifth, minor seventh, minor ninth, Perfect eleventh and minor thirteenth.

F#7b9b13   Notes: F# - A# - C# - E - G - B - D Intervals: 1 3 5 b7 b9 11 b13

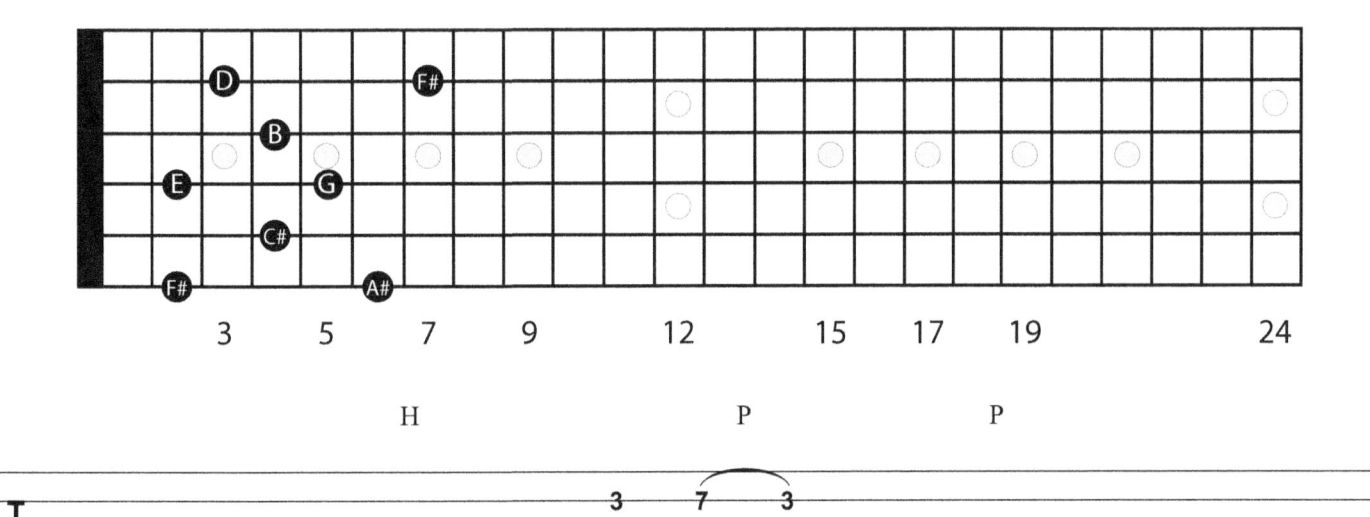

Example 6 is a Gmaj13#9#11 arpeggio based on the sixth mode of the Harmonic minor Scale; Lydian #2, and consists of the intervals Root, Major third, Perfect fifth, Major seventh, augmented ninth, Perfect eleventh and minor thirteenth.

Gmaj13#9#11   Notes: G - B - D - F# - A# - C# - E Intervals: 1 3 5 7 #9 #11 13

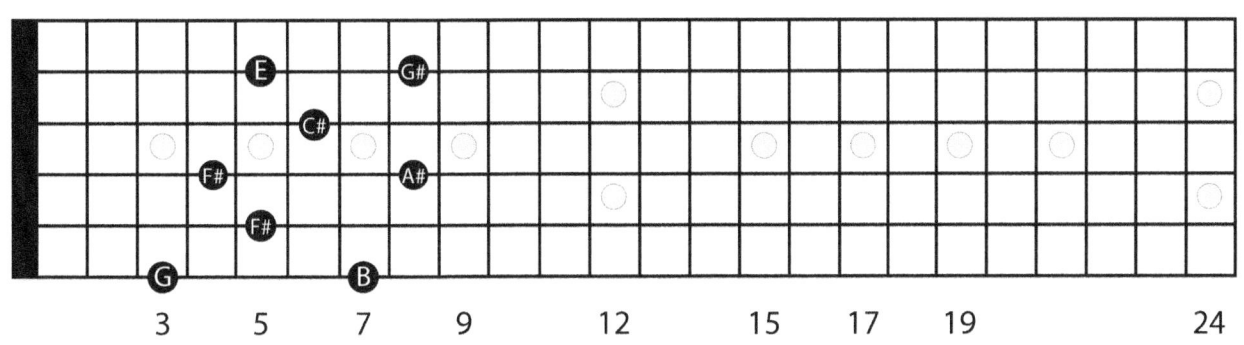

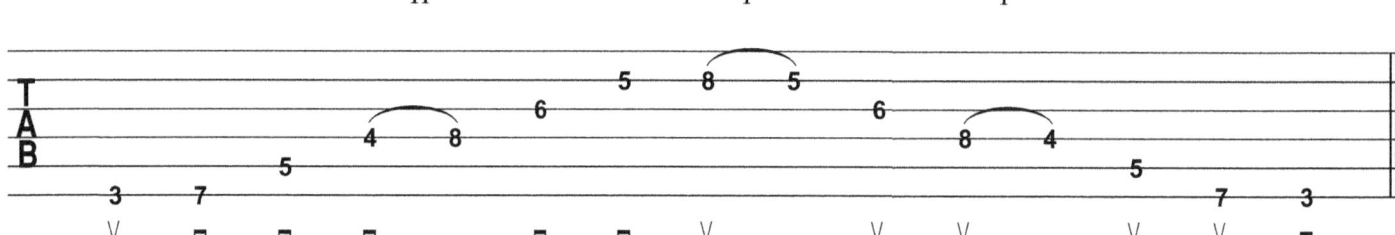

Example 7 is a A#dimb13b9b11 arpeggio based on the seventh mode of the Harmonic minor Scale; Mixolydian #1, and consists of the intervals Root, minor third, diminished fifth, minor seventh, minor ninth, diminished eleventh and Major thirteenth.

A#dim^{b13b9b11} **Notes: A#-C#-E-G-B-D-F# Intervals: 1 ♭3 ♭5 ♭7 ♭9 ♭11 ♭13**

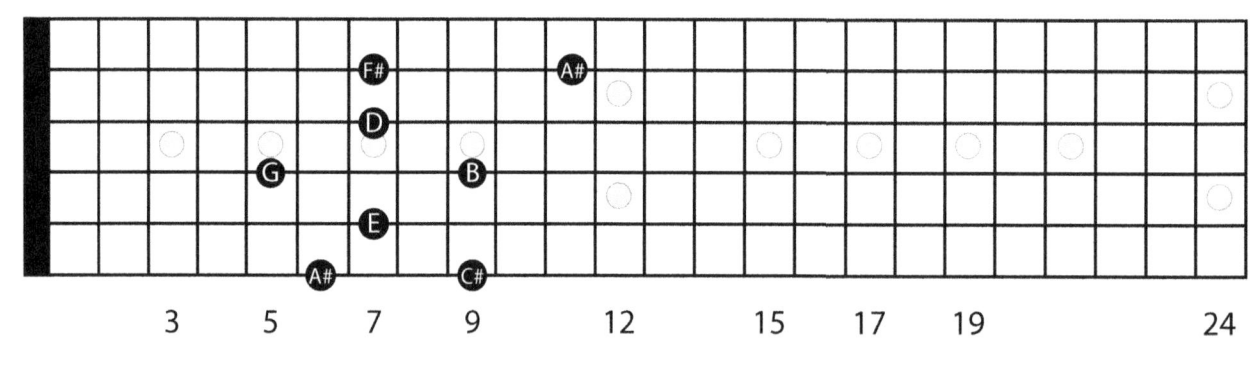

50

Chapter 13:
Four String 5ths Arpeggios

In this lesson we are going to look at four string arpeggios that based primarily on intervals of a fifth. The technique used in these arpeggios will use a down sweep motion and an up sweep motion causing the first and last notes to be played twice.

Example 1 starts on C at the 10th fret of the 4th string. This is going to be based on C Lydian, the fourth mode of the G Major scale. The basic concept is just like the last example, however Rusty will throw in different notes of the mode in no specific order as he usually uses these when doing free-form improvisation. The diagram below (as in all of the following examples) shows the fifths shape on strings 4, 3, 2 and 1 but also shows the other scale notes he opts for on the 1st string. In example one he uses the 2nd, 3rd and augmented 4th on the 1st string and alternates between them while sweeping the four strings.

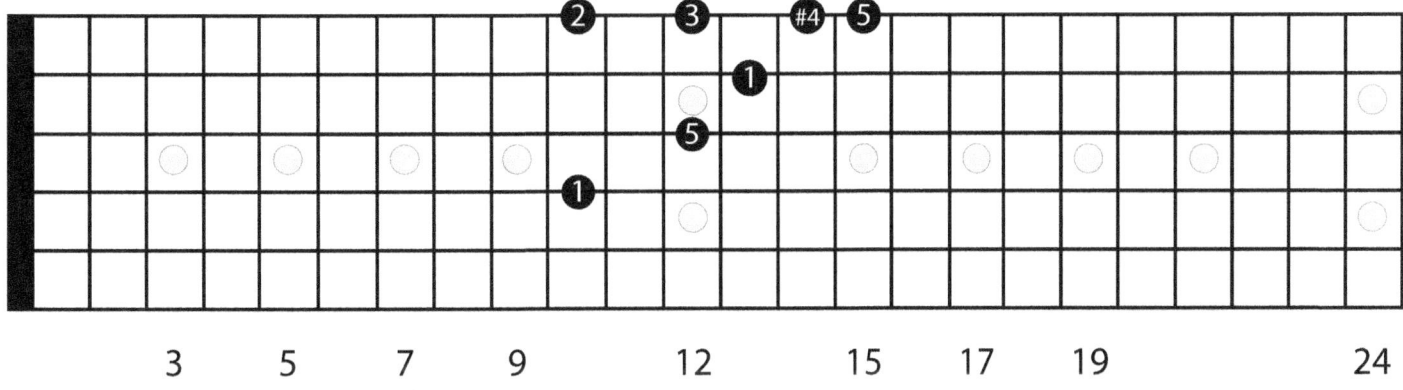

Example 2 is based on the D Mixolydian mode and incorporates the 2nd, 3rd and 4th degrees of the mode.

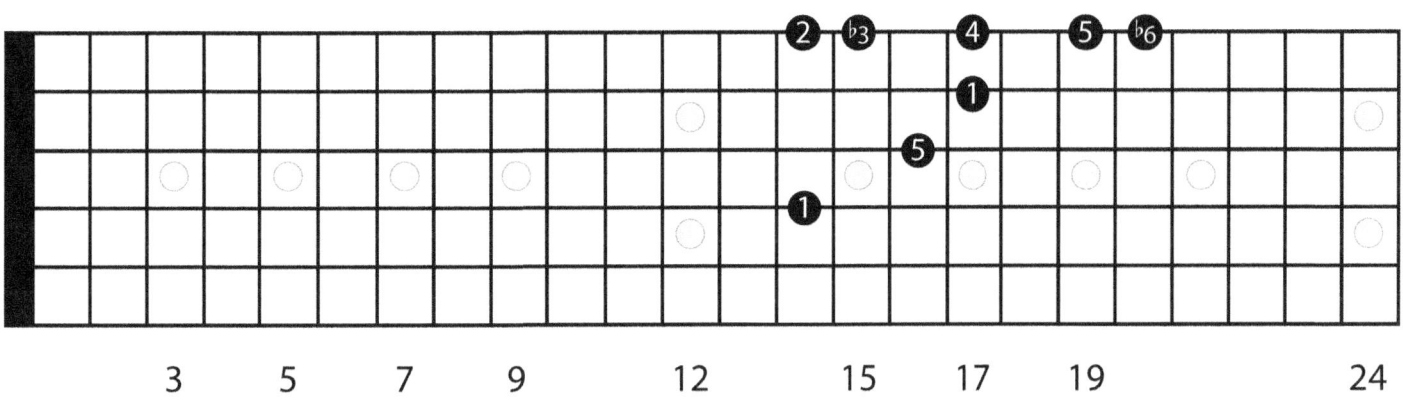

Example 3 is based on the E Aeolian mode and incorporates the 2nd, minor 3rd, 4th and minor 6th degrees of the mode.

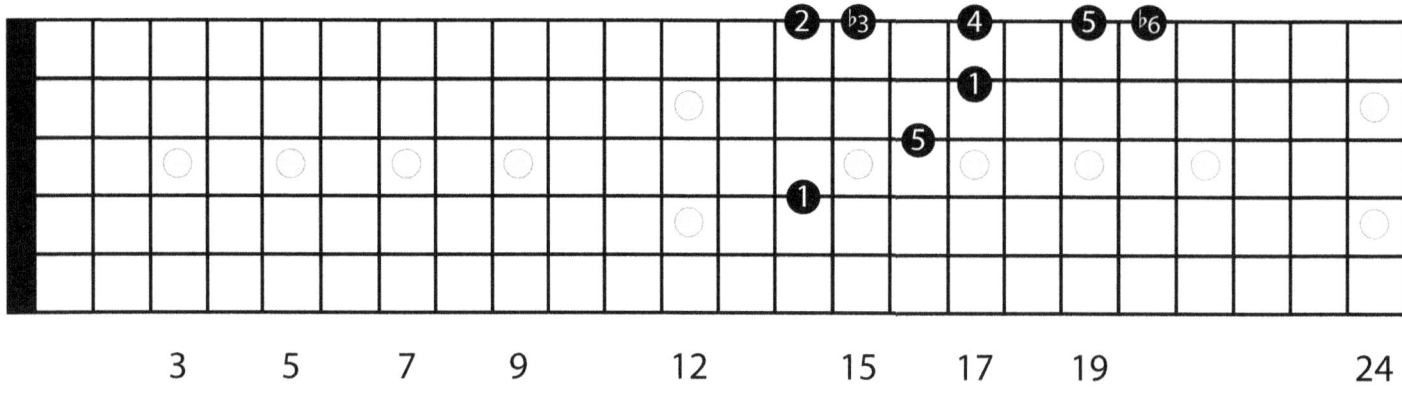

Example 4 is based on the G Ionian mode (G Major Scale) and incorporates the 2nd, 3rd and 4th degrees of the mode.

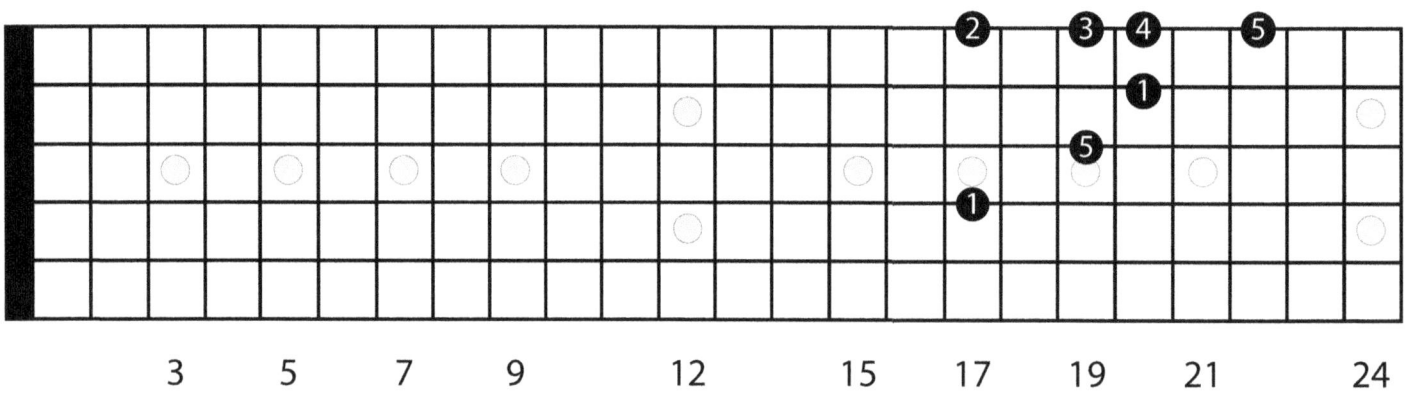

Example 5 is based on the A Dorian mode and uses the 2nd, minor 3rd and 4th degrees of the mode.

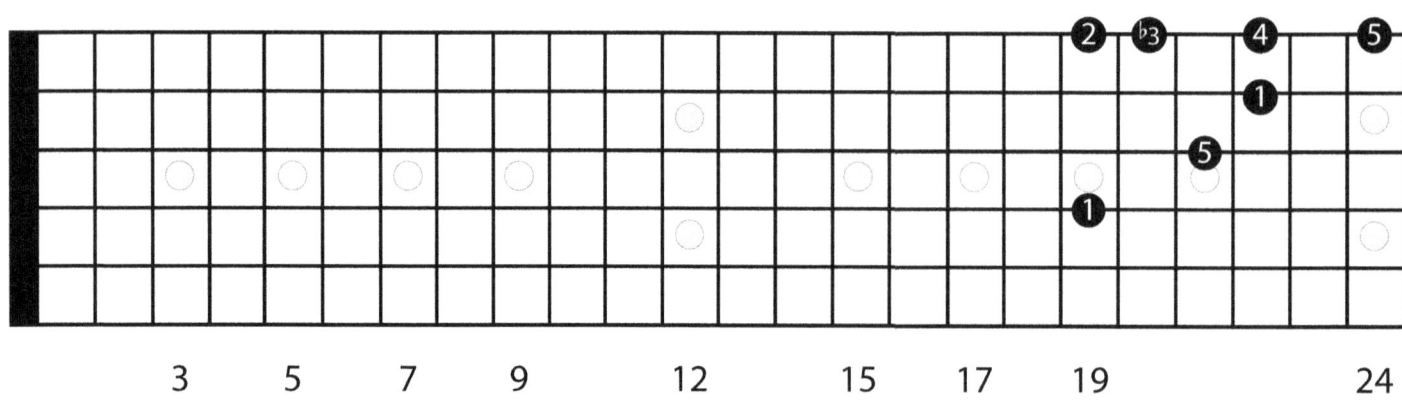

Example 6 is based on the E Phrygian mode and utilizes the minor 2nd, minor 3rd and 4th degrees of the mode.

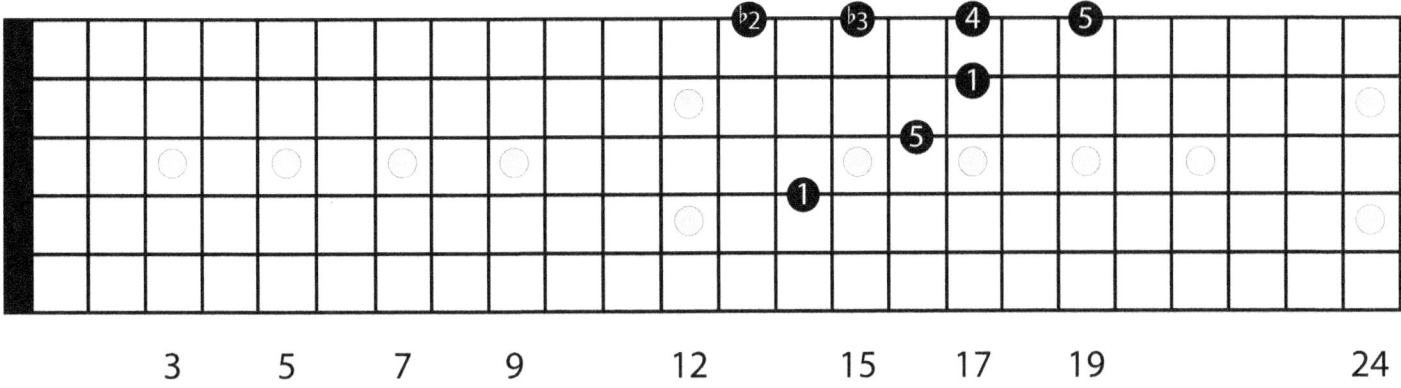

Chapter 14: Sweeping 5ths Key of "C" Major

The next example we are going to cover is taking the sweeping 5ths concept we just learned in the last lesson and putting them together in the key of "C" Major. In the Key of "C" Major the chords are C5, D5, E5, F5, G5 and A5. The example starts on the D5 chord. Notice that all of the position changes occur with your pinkie on the first string.

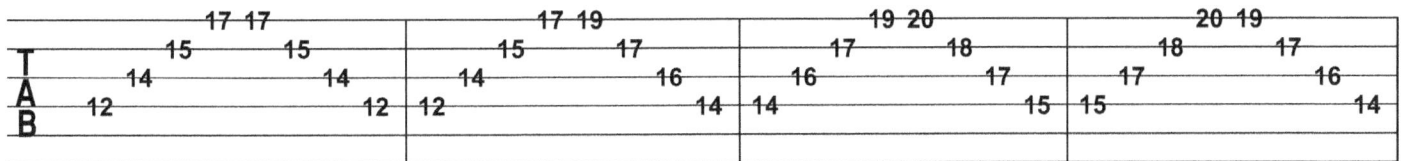

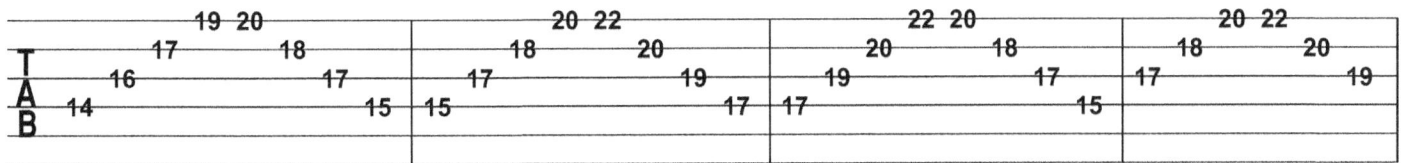

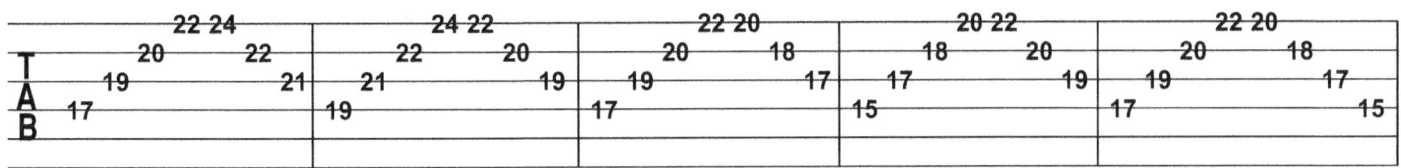

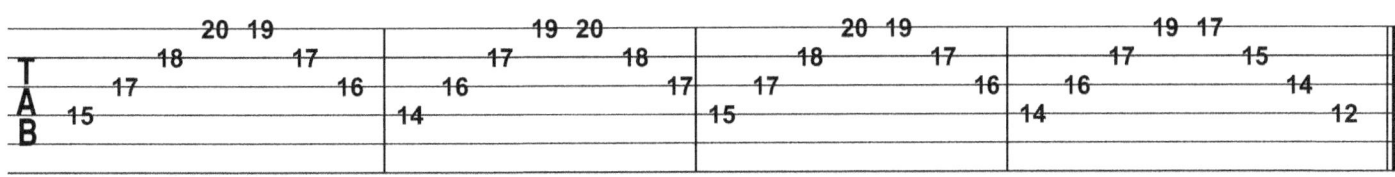

Chapter 15: Two String Sweep Picking Arpeggio Sequence

As simple as the title of this lesson may sound, two-string sweeping is a bit tricky to get the separation of the notes. The picking concept is one down stroke across two strings, and one up stroke across two strings. The tricky part is getting your fretting hand to pivot across two strings. In the example below Rusty is playing the 15th fret of the 1st and 2nd strings with his 1st finger. Once he plays the 2nd string, he rolls his finger so it releases pressure off of the 2nd string and then applies pressure to the 1st string. This keeps the notes from bleeding together and sounding separately. It is important to note that you will have some level of bleed between the notes as compared to more conventional 3, 4, 5 and 6 string sweeping patterns and licks, but you want to try to keep the "bleed" to a minimum. In the fifth and final section Rusty will use three string sweeping arpeggios.

First Section

Em

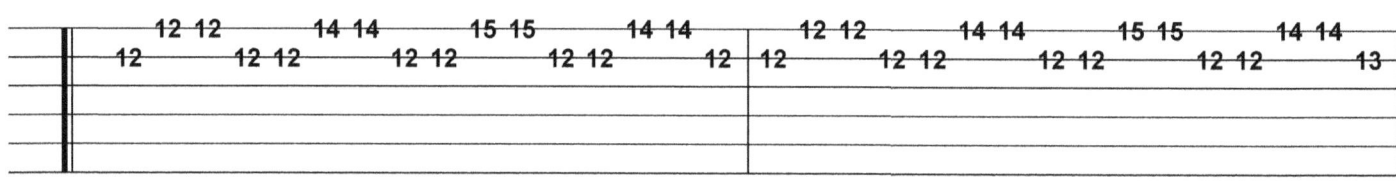

C

C#°

First & Second Section "tie."

D

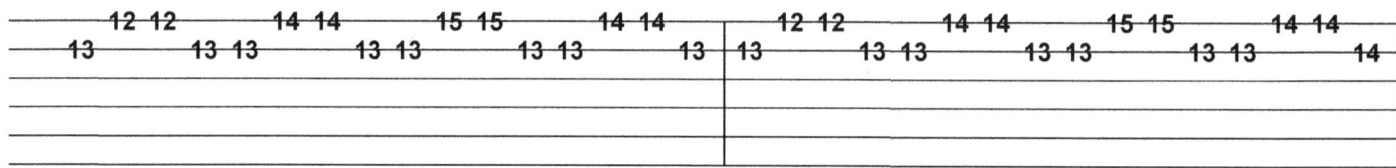
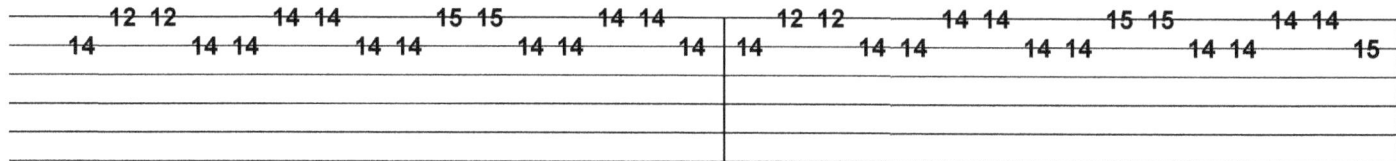

D#o

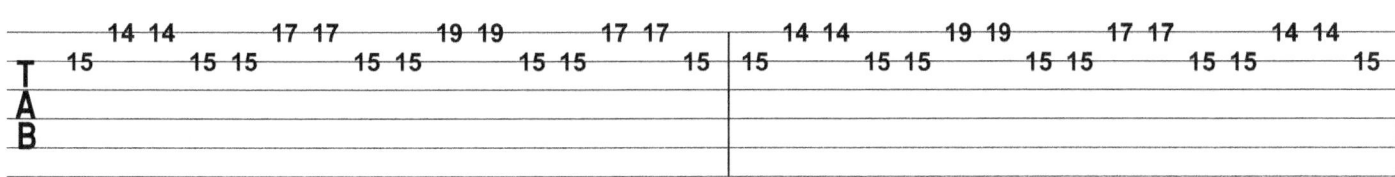

Second Section

Em

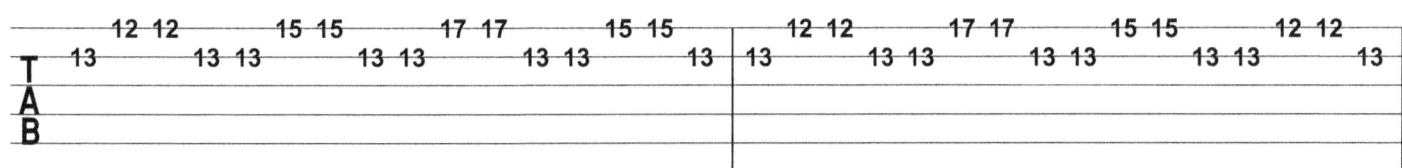

D

C

D

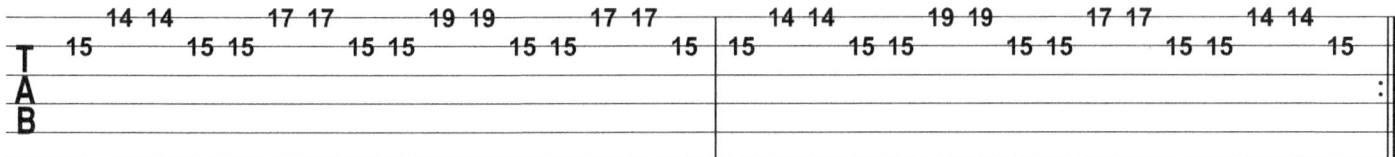

Third Section - Lydian Section *(entire section played twice)*

Cadd9#11   C

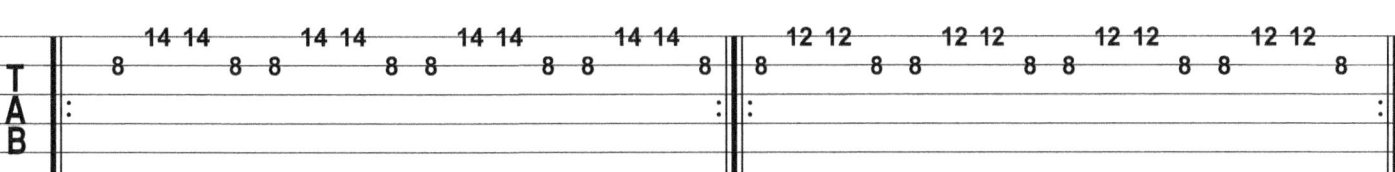

Bsus4   Bm

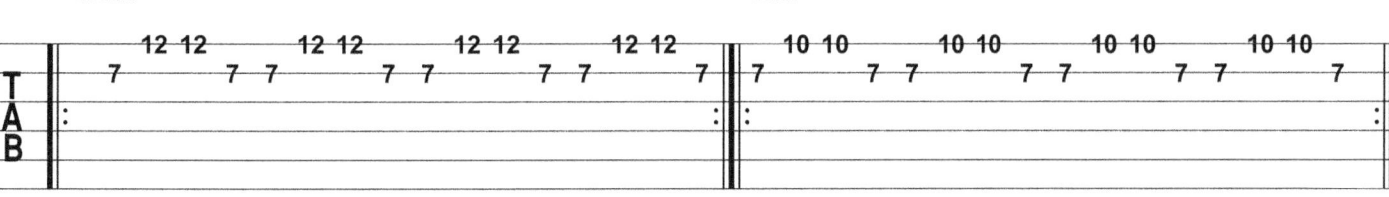

Fourth Section

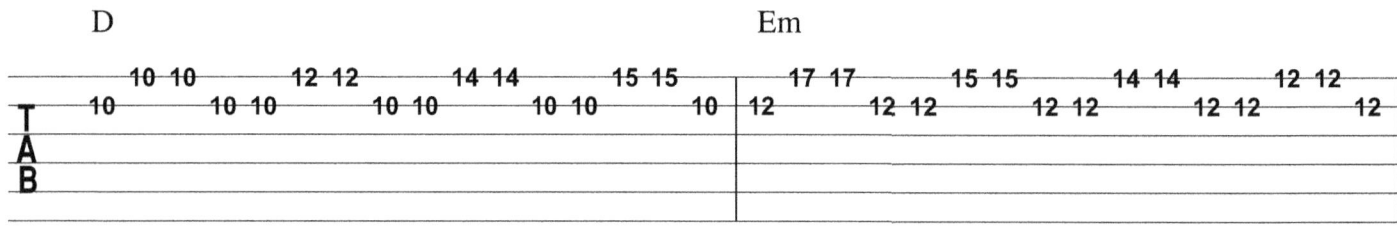

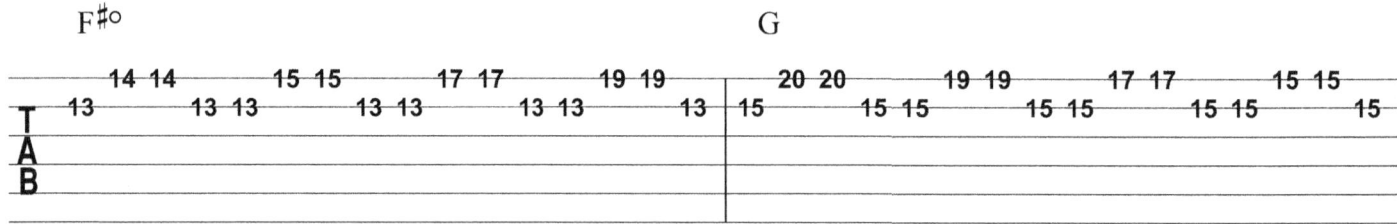

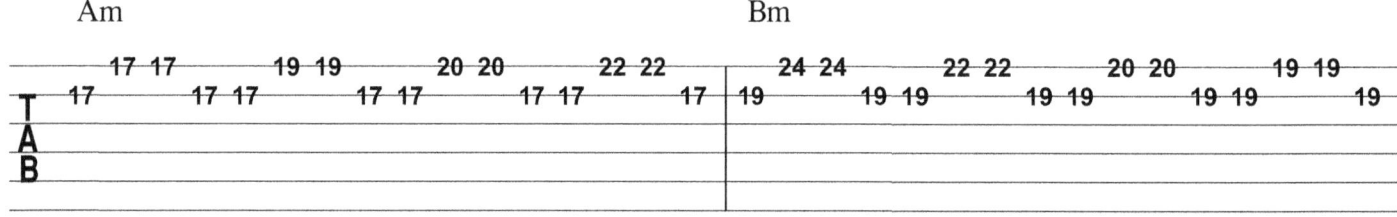

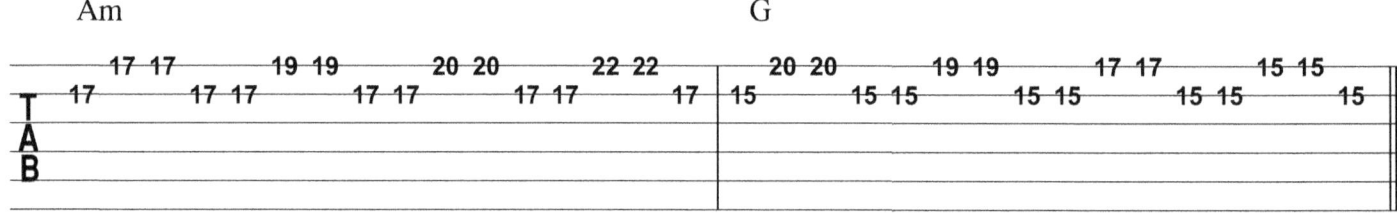

Fifth Section

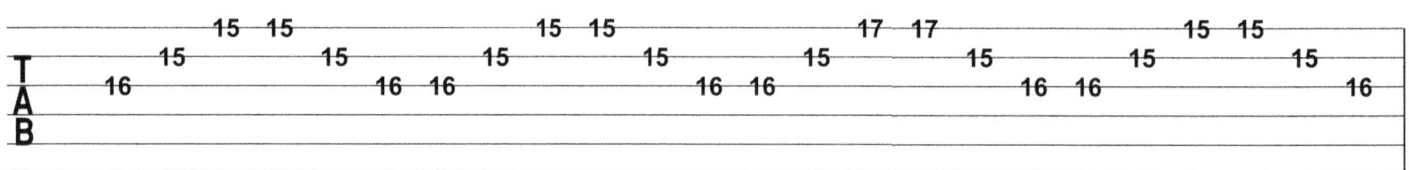

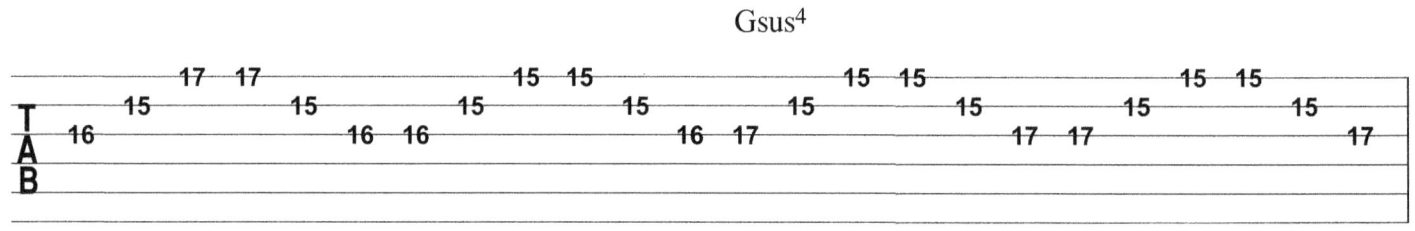

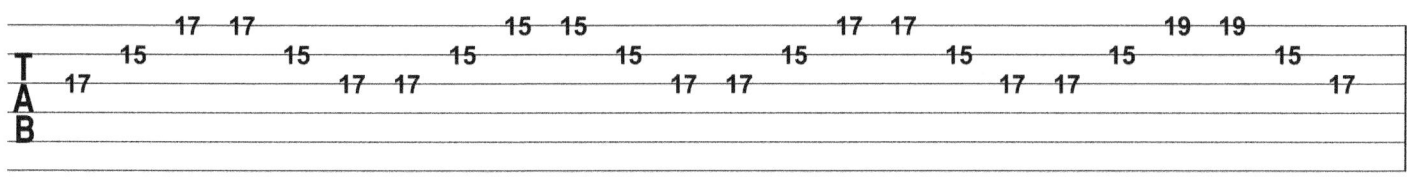

Am

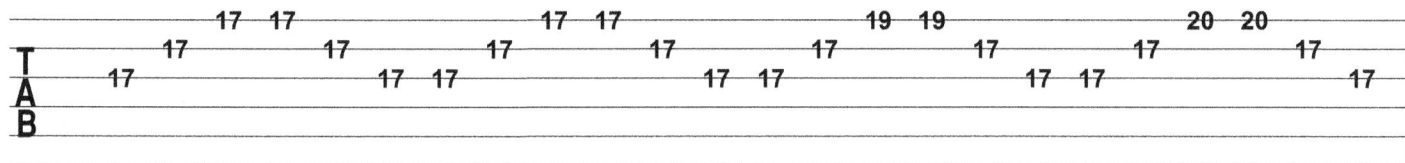

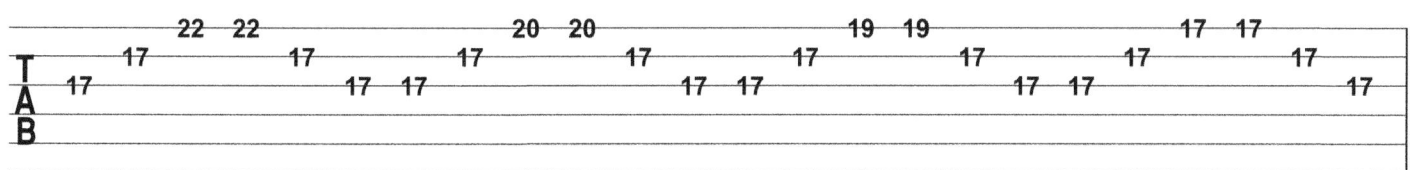

Bm

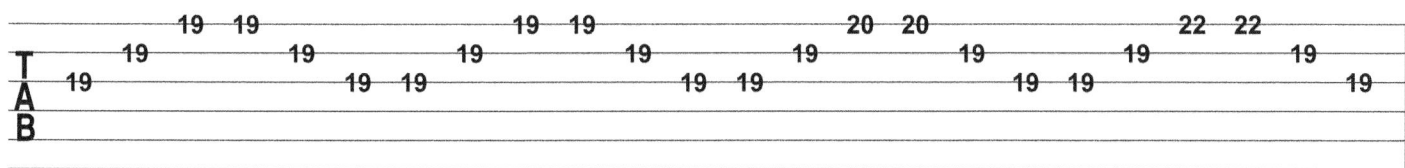

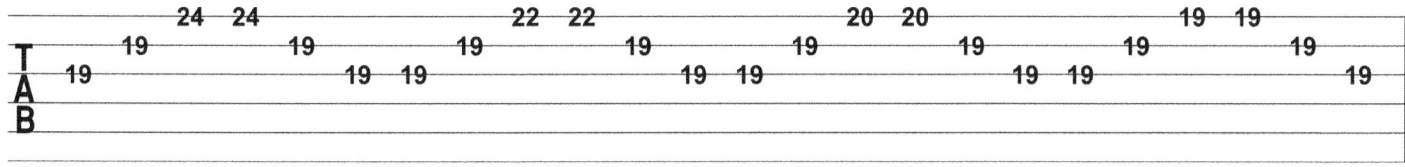

Chapter 16: Two-String Economy Picking Arpeggio Sequence

Economy picking is very similar to sweep picking in the fact that you are still using a "sweeping" motion, but only when changing from string to string. For example, the sequence starts on the 2nd string 12th fret with an up stroke, then goes to the 17th fret of the 2nd string with a down stroke and sweeps to the 1st string for the third note in the sequence on the 15th fret on the 1st string. The concept is to plan ahead so that you wind up with a continuous sweeping motion from string to string and then use alternate picking for the other notes that are played in a linear fashion.

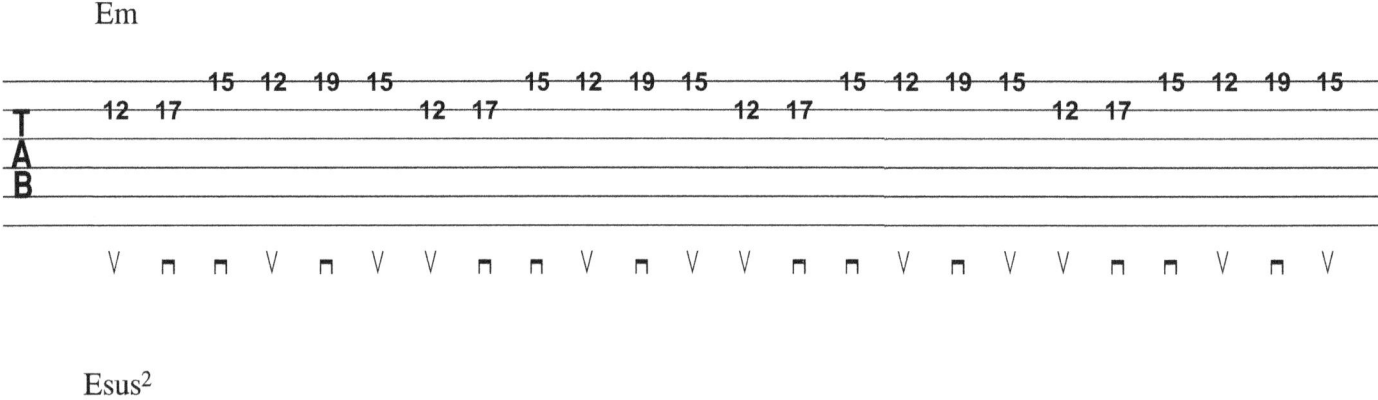

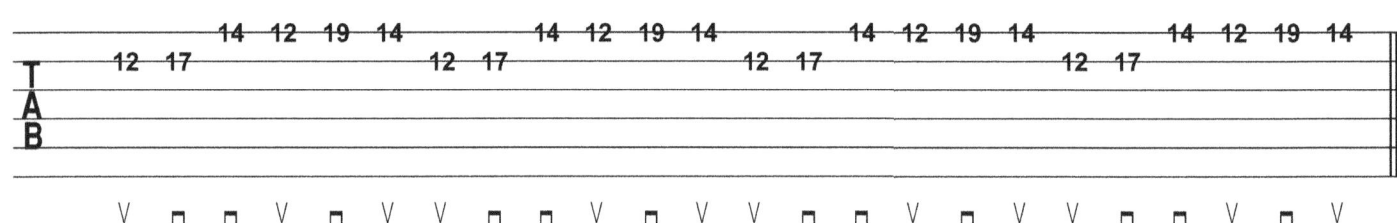

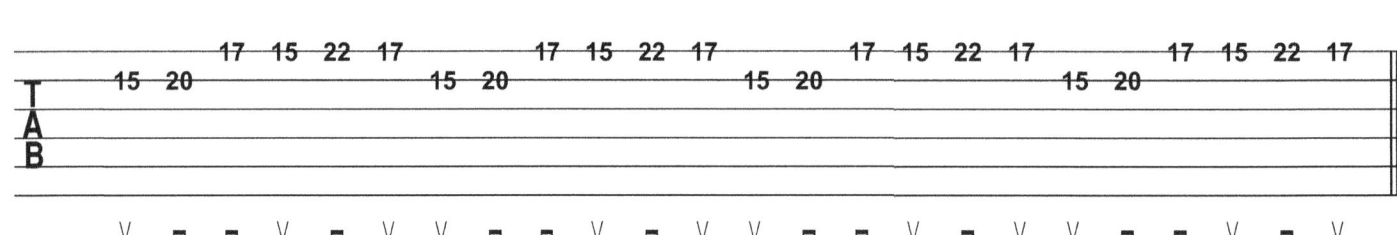

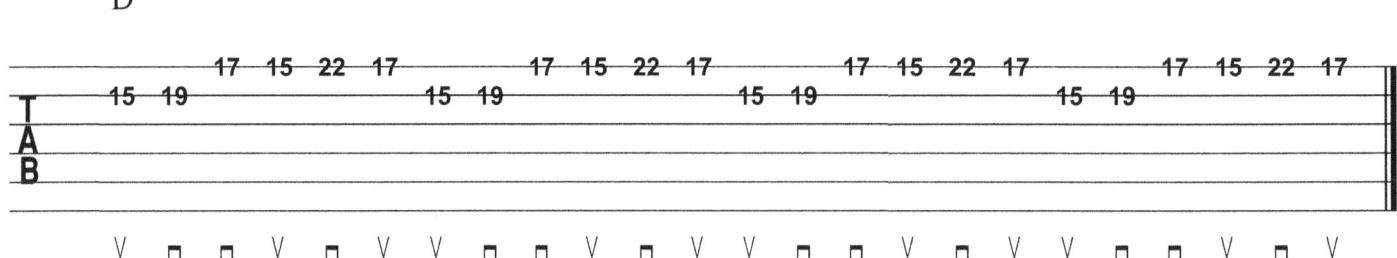

Am

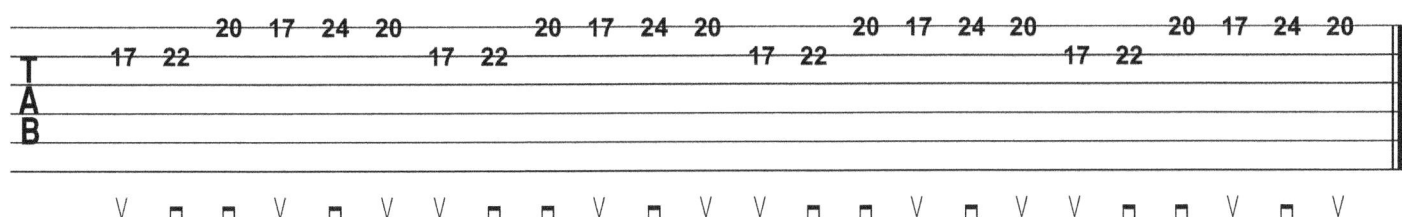

Asus²

Chapter 17:
Diminished 7th Arpeggios Sweep Picking

Rusty employs the use of Diminished arpeggios in a Phrygian Dominant (also known as Phrygian Major) application. Phrygian Dominant is the 5th mode of the harmonic minor scale and derives a dominant 7th chord in within a four part harmony structure (Root, Major Third, Perfect Fifth and a minor Seventh). In the key of "E" Harmonic Minor the V chord is B7 derived from B Phrygian Major. The examples that follow are derived from the E Harmonic Minor context employing ideas based on the B Phrygian Dominant setting.

Example 1 illustrates the symmetrical nature of the Diminished Seventh arpeggio. Each time the arpeggio inverts as it moves across the neck, the fingering patterns remain the same which gives the arpeggio its symmetry.

The most important thing to keep in the back of your mind is that the shapes repeat every minor third (one and a half steps) on the neck, the only difference is the order of the notes.

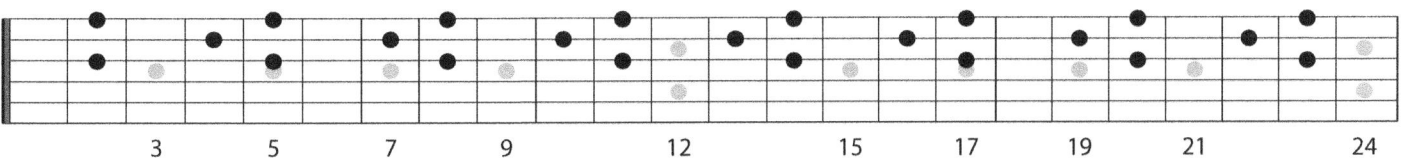

Examples 2, 3 and **4** will look at different ideas using the diminished 7th arpeggio on strings 1, 2 and 3.

Ex. 2   **Ex. 3**   **Ex. 4**

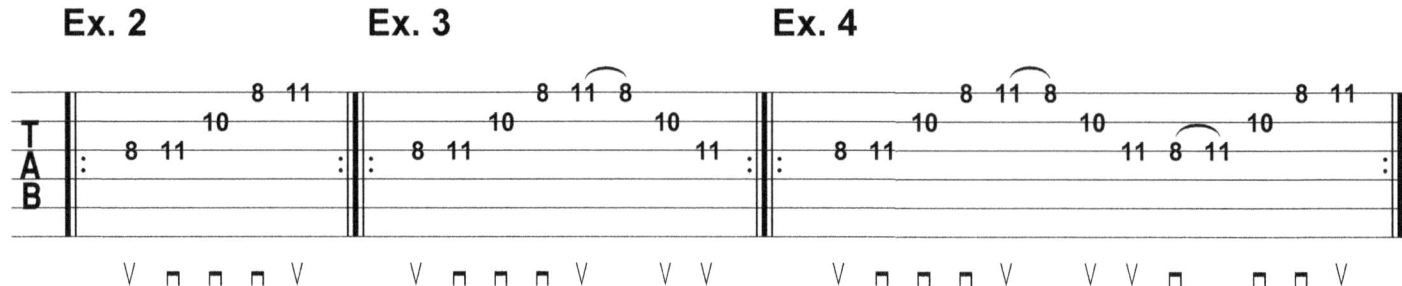

Example 5 Illustrates the Diminished arpeggio symmetry on strings 2, 3 and 4.

Ex. 5

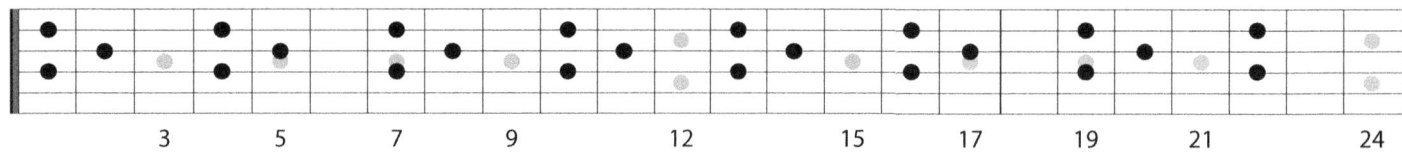

Examples 6 and **7** will look at different ideas using the diminished 7th arpeggio on strings 2, 3 and 4. **Examples 8** and **9** will use a shape from the second grouping and a shape from the first grouping together.

Ex. 6   **Ex. 7**   **Ex. 8**

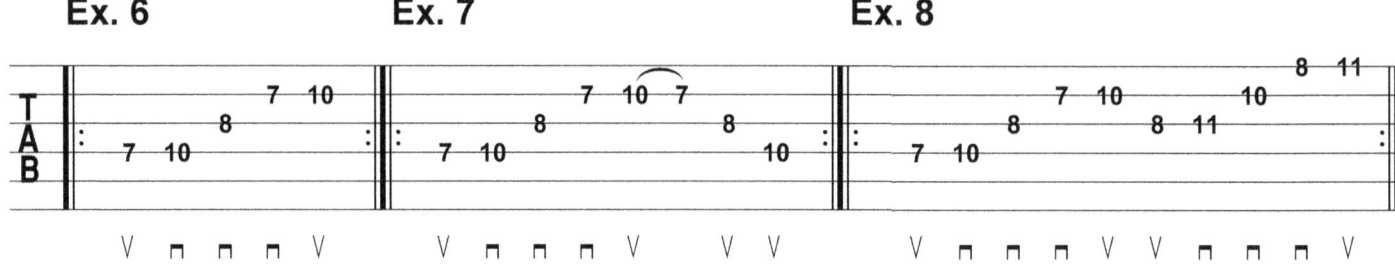

Ex. 9

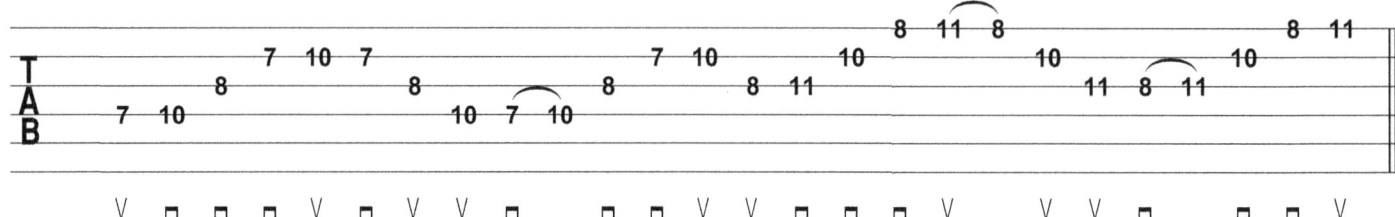

Examples 10, 11 and 12 will use the diminished "shape" patterns across all six strings.

Ex. 10

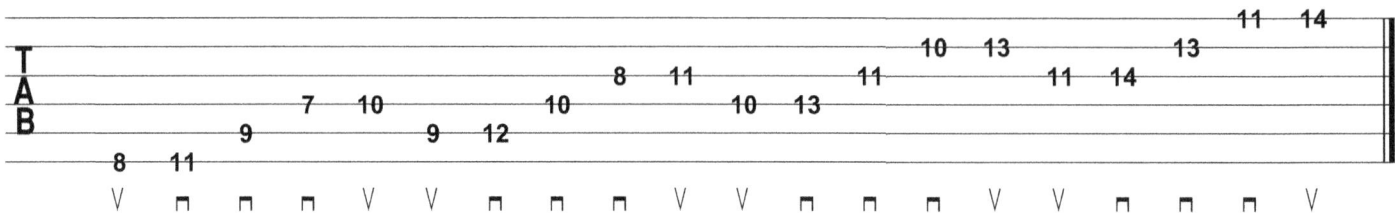

60

Ex. 11

Ex. 12

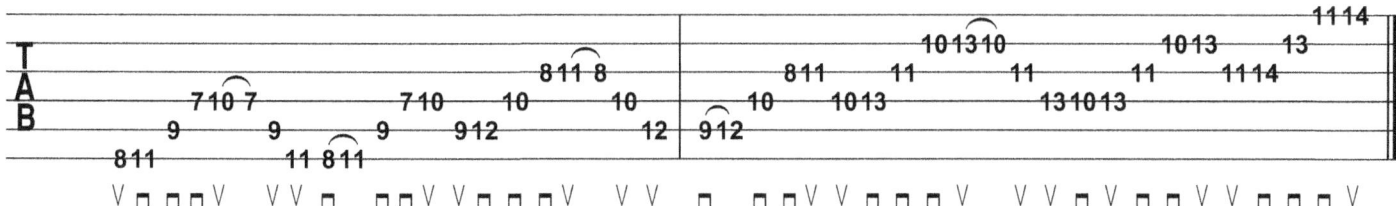

Chapter 18: Applying Diminished 7th Arpeggios Using Legato

Before we get into the use of legato in the following examples, it is important to know that when Rusty is playing legato he ONLY picks on the first note of the ascending strings and uses legato (hammer ons and pull offs) for all descending strings. Play the following D major scale example to see this technique in action.

Examples 1 through 4 will employ string skipping with legato to play the diminished seventh arpeggios. Even though Rusty is skipping strings, he still does not pick any of the descending strings, they will be sounded by hammering your finger onto the notes.

Ex. 1

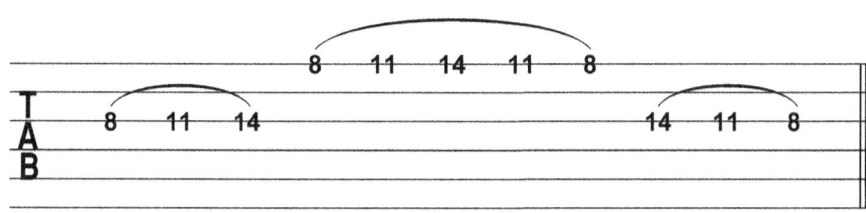

Ex. 2 *(Shifting positions with example 1)*

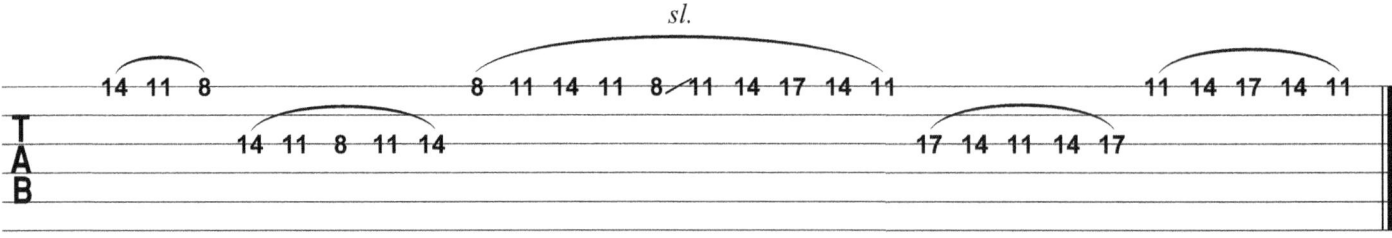

Ex. 3 *(Using string groupings)*

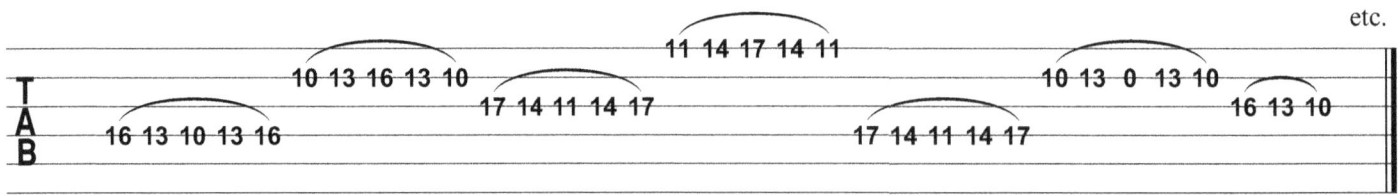

Ex. 4 *(Shifting positions with example 3)*

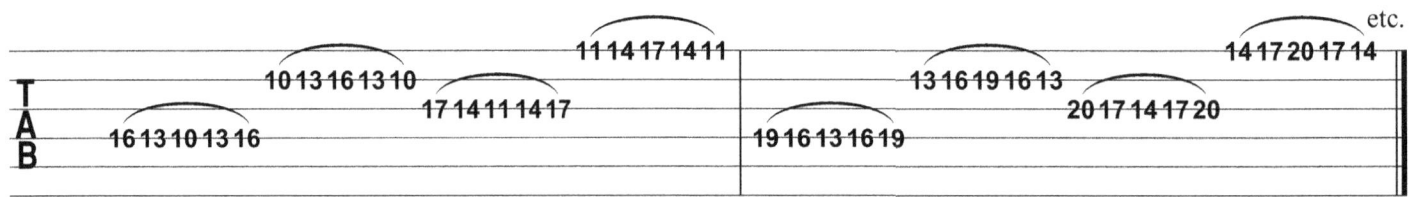

In **Example 5**, Rusty taps using both the ring and middle fingers of his picking hand. Above the tab you will notice a "T2" and a "T3." The T2 signifies tapping with your picking hand middle finger and the T3 signifies tapping with your picking hand ring finger.

**Note that you can stay on one string in one position and practice this multi-finger tap legato roll before trying the whole example if you find it difficult at first. So you would just start off by practicing.

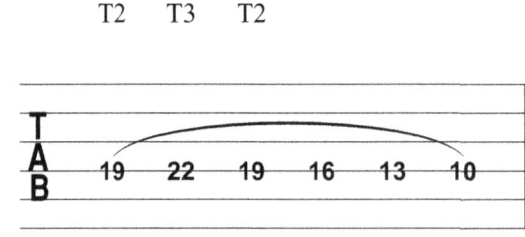

Ex. 5 *(Multi-finger tapping)*

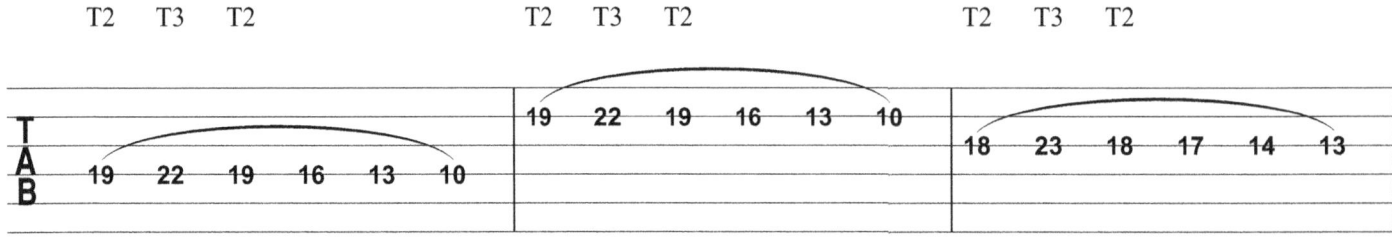

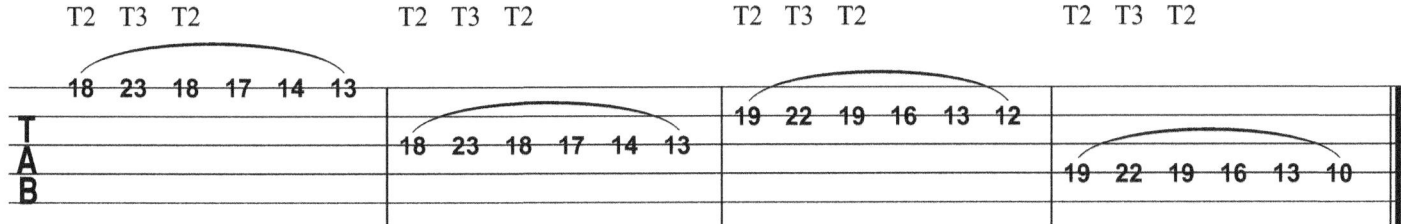

Chapter 19: Three Octave String Skipping Legato Arpeggios

One of the biggest misconceptions made by guitarists that are new to playing arpeggios is that they are only played with sweep picking. That is hardly the case, they can be played using just about any technique; alternate picking, legato, hammer ons, pull offs, tapping etc. The following lessons are going to start branching out into these different types of approaches to playing arpeggios.

The first technique we are going to look at is playing three octave arpeggios in **Example 1** using string skipping and legato. There are some wide stretches and the fingering used is imperative as each position shift is strategic in order to set you up for the next stretch in the sequence.

Ex. 1

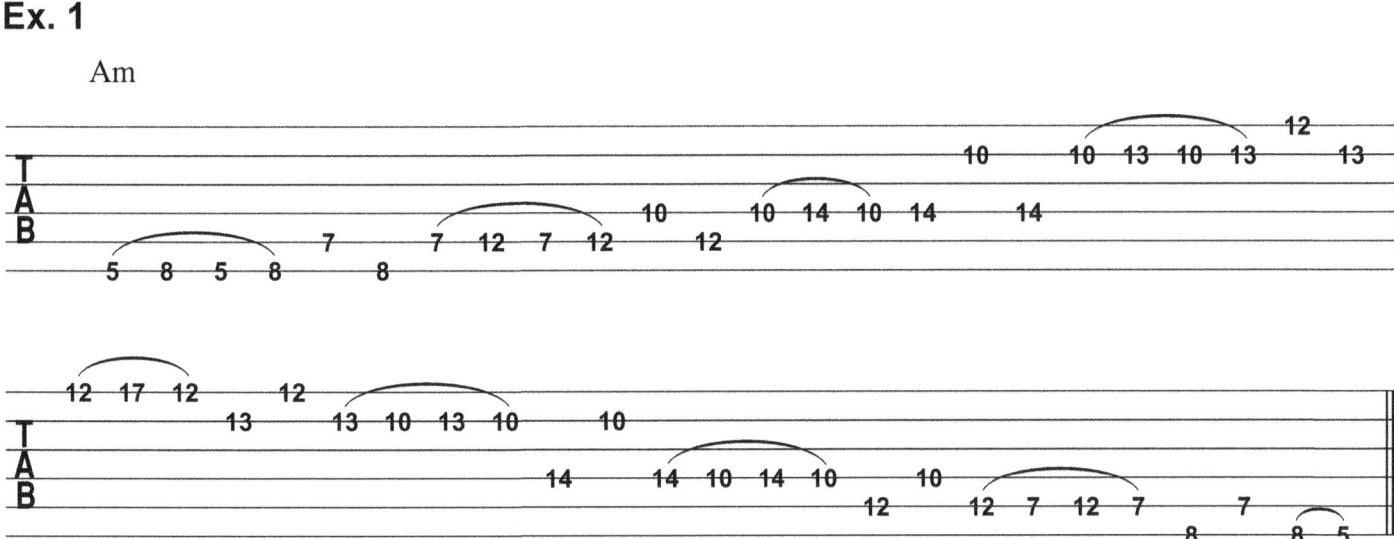

Examples 2, 3 and **4** will utilize the same sequence but now will be played through diminished, major and augmented arpeggios.

Ex. 2

B°

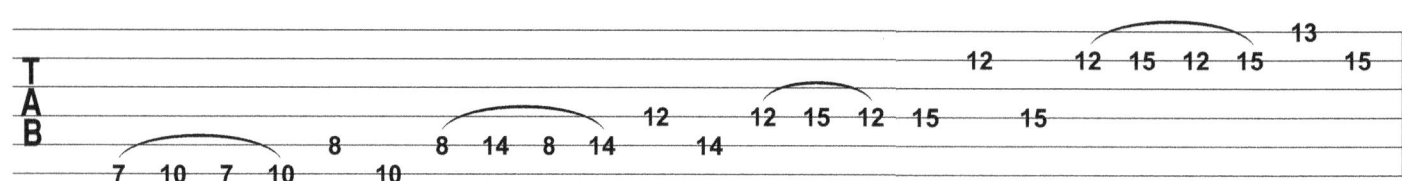

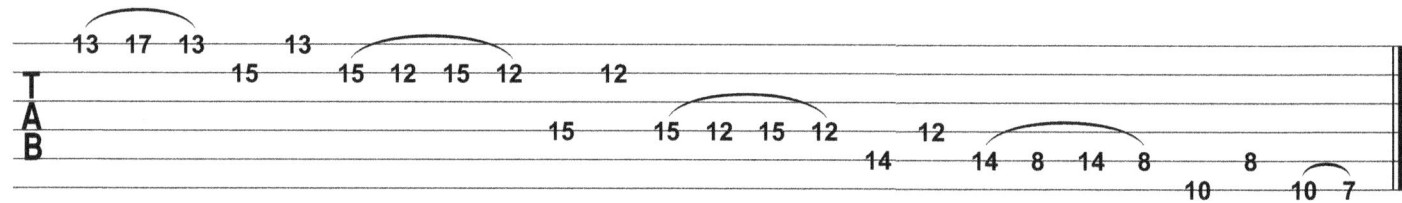

Ex. 3

C

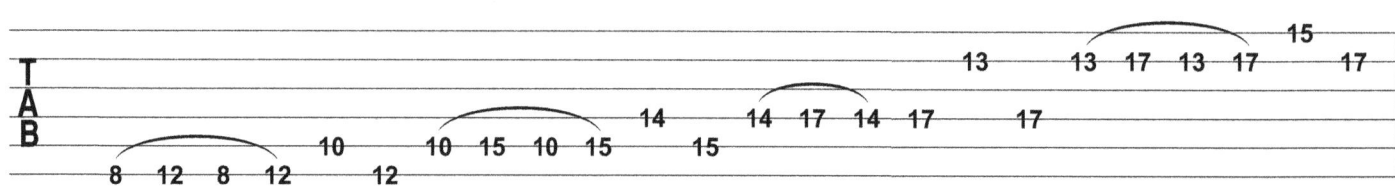

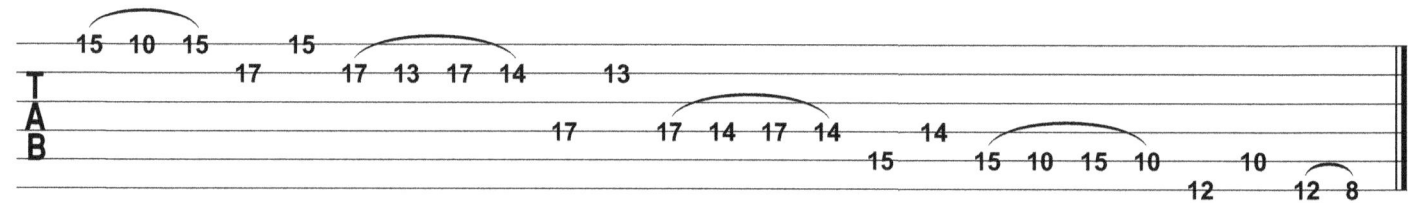

Ex. 4

Caug

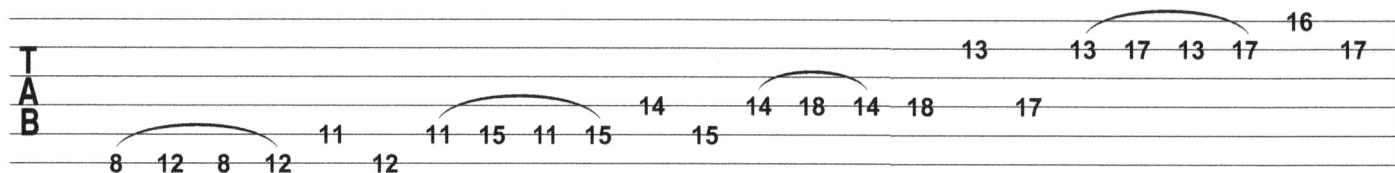

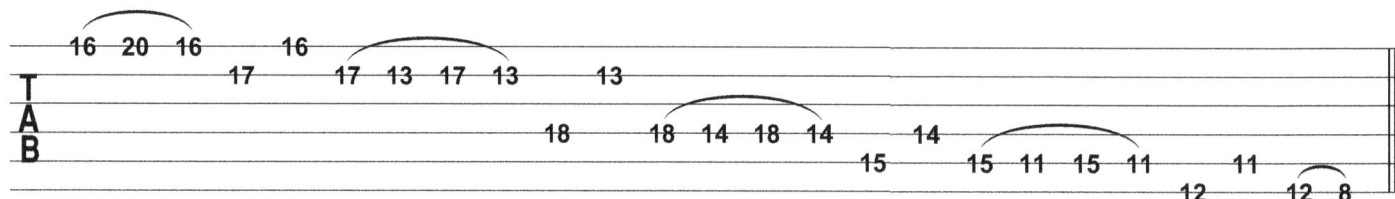

Chapter 20:
Three Octave Arpeggios with Tapping

In this section Rusty covers three octave 6 string arpeggios that will incorporate legato, sweep picking and tapping all at the same time. The ideas will all start with a tap for the highest note of the arpeggio and descend all six strings without any picking and then will have a four string sweep in the ascension of the arpeggios.

Ex. 1

Ex. 2

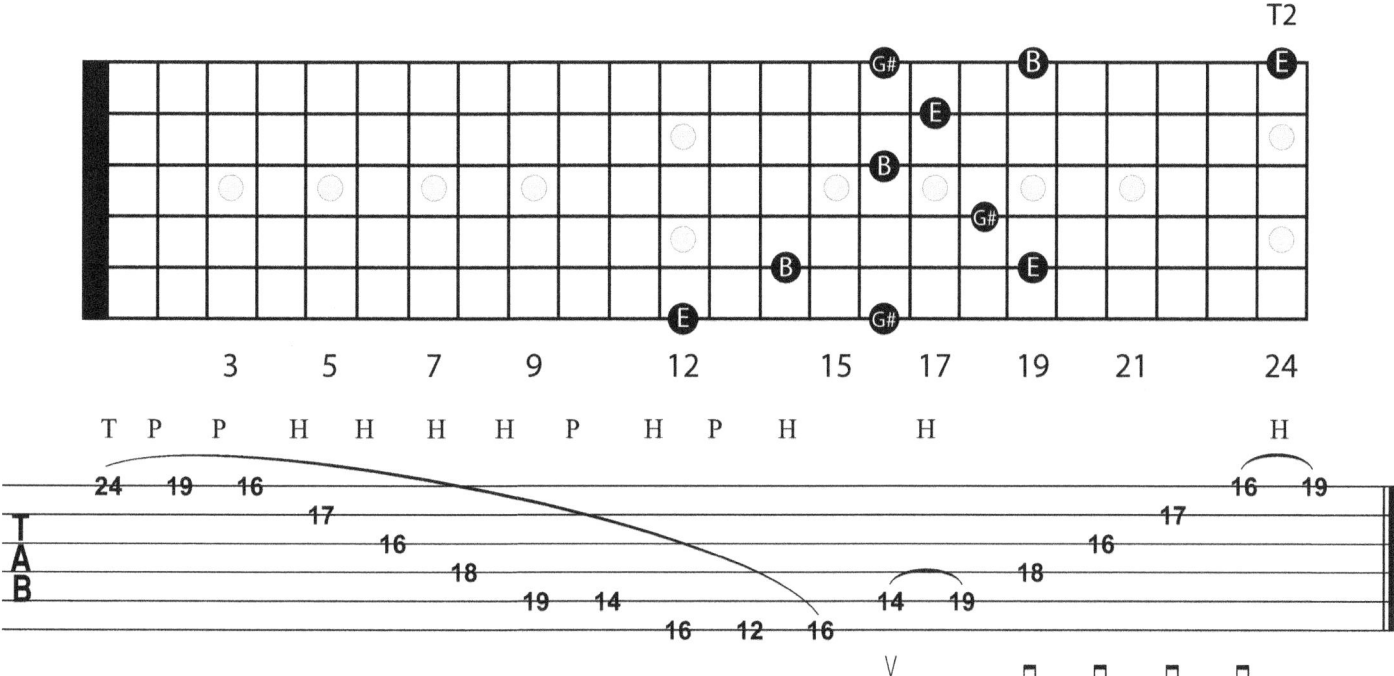

65

Ex. 3

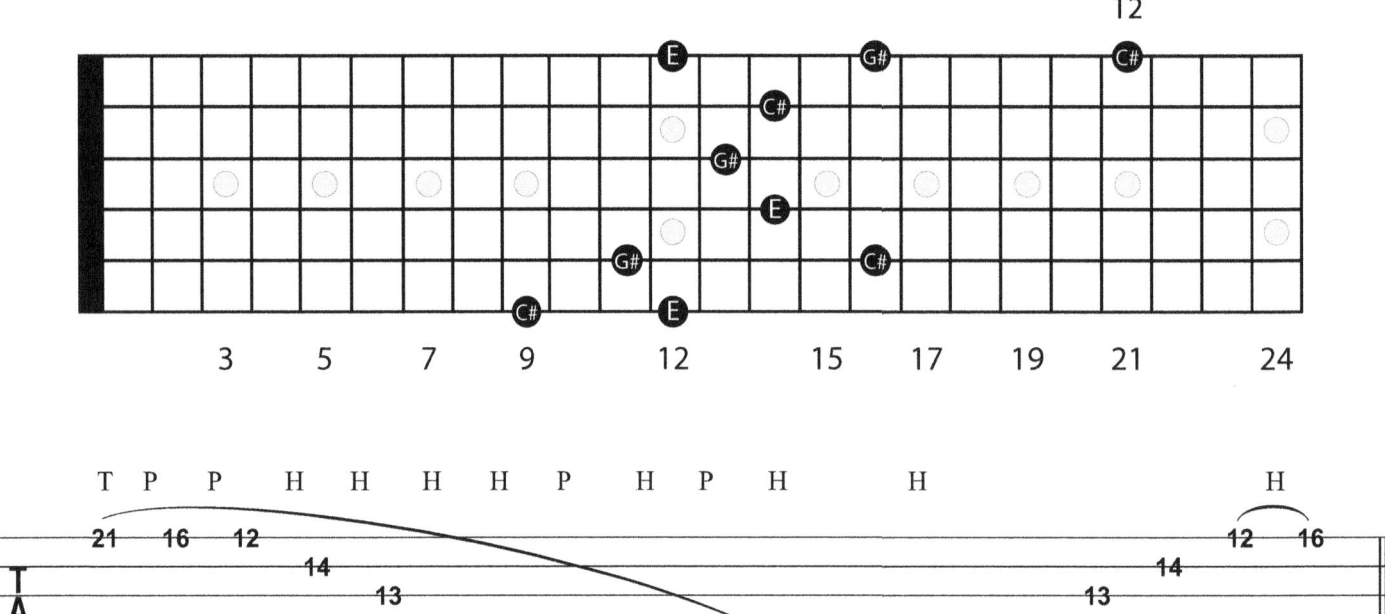

Once you have these three arpeggio fingerings memorized, you can apply them to any diatonic Major chord scale. All you need to know is this chord scale formula:

I - IV - V chords are Major

ii - iii - vi are minor

vii is diminished

Now you can take that formula and apply it to any diatonic major scale and work out the arpeggios for that key. For example, in the key of "G" Major (G - A - B - C - D - E - F#) you would play:

G Major - A minor - B minor - C Major - D Major - E minor - F#diminished

Chapter 21: String Skipping Legato Solo

In this lesson Rusty takes you through a string skipping legato solo. Before we begin lets look at the arpeggios that will be used in this example:

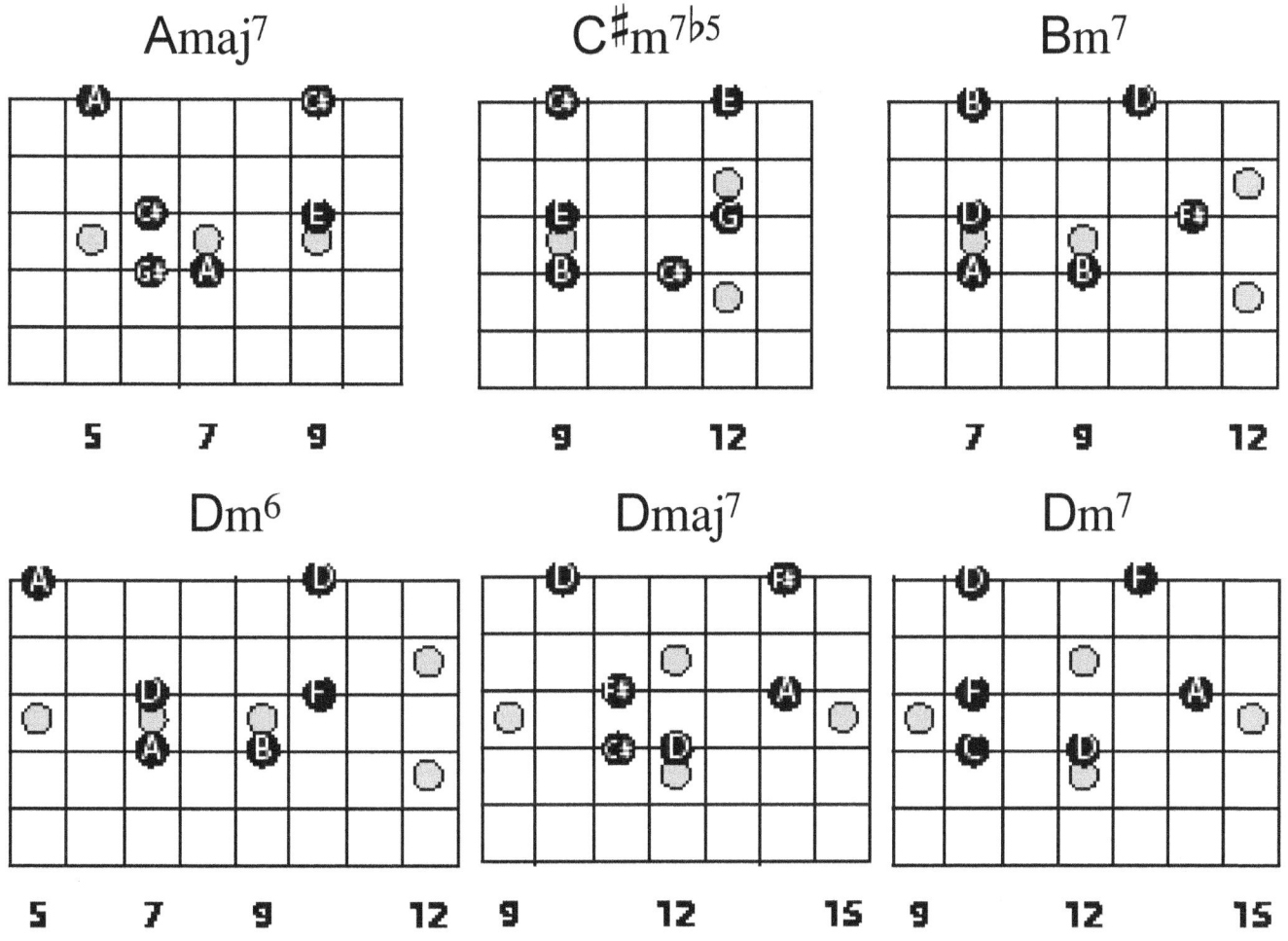

Now lastly before we begin, lets look at the sequence that will be applied to all of the arpeggios in this solo:

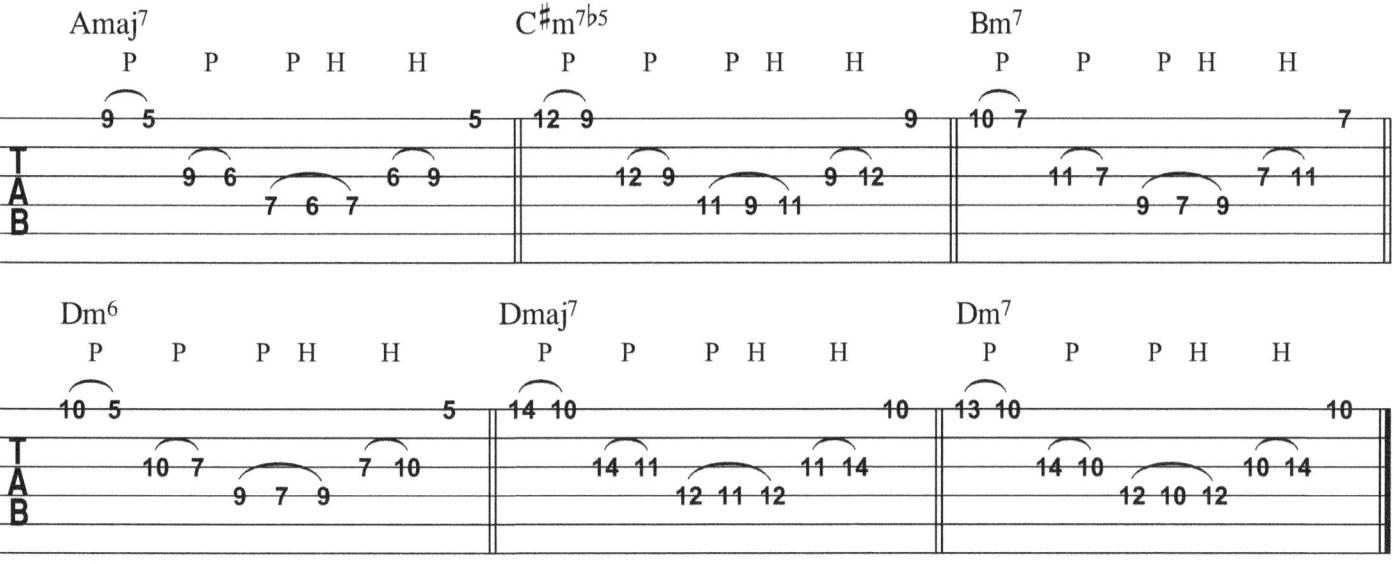

Here is the eight bar solo. Make sure to only pick ascending legato pieces, descending legato sections are performed with the fretting hand fingers using only hammer ons and pull offs we just covered in the legato lessons of this program.

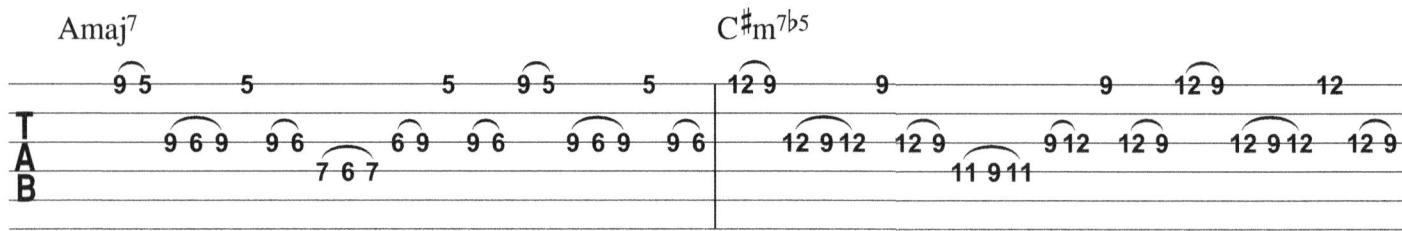

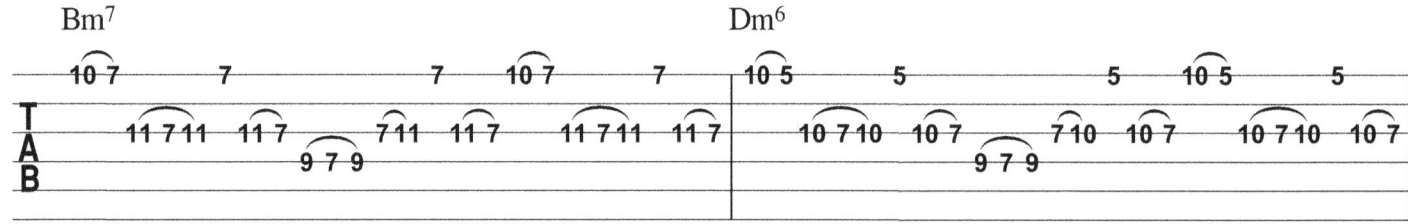

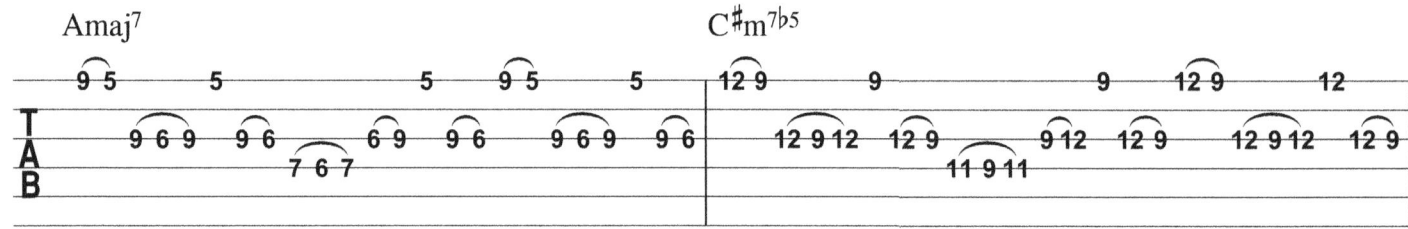

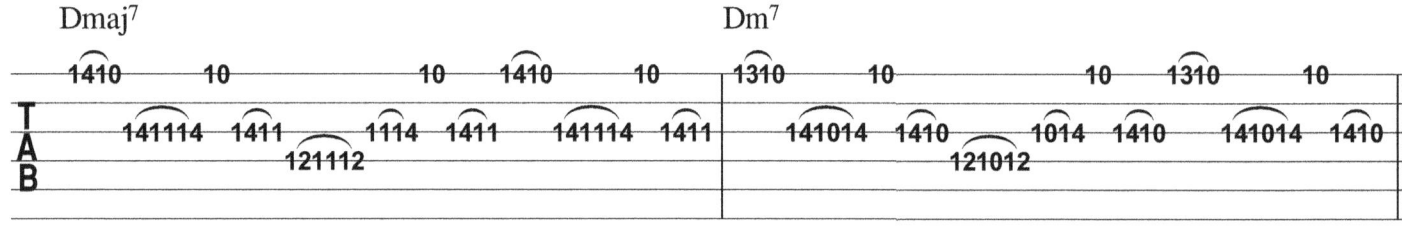

Bonus Lessons

Chapter 22:
Single String Triads "Death Licks"

This lesson on Single String Triads is one of Rusty's favorite subjects to cover. And note that it is strongly recommended that you spend some time warming up your left hand prior to working on these concepts, there are some pretty massive stretches that will require your hands to be loosened up and ready to handle such requirements.

In each one of the following examples each string will have a triad based off of the 12th fret. The triads (arpeggios) we will look at will be derived right from the E minor scale:

CHORD

INTERVAL		Em	F#m7b5	Gmaj	Am	Bm	Cmaj	Dmaj
	Root	E	F#	G	A	B	C	D
	Third	G b3	A b3	B 3	C b3	D b3	E 3	F# 3
	Fifth	B 5	C b5	D 5	E 5	F# 5	G 5	A 5

Use the "Em Chord Scale Chart" above to aid you in understanding the seven diatonic chords and their chord tones while learning this lesson.

The first triad we will be looking at is E minor starting on the 12th fret of the 6th string. The intervals are Root - E, minor third - G and Perfect fifth B. The intervals will be played on the 12th, 15th and 19th frets of the 6th string.

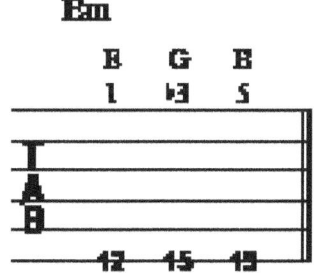

The rest of the triads we will look at in the twelfth position are A minor, D Major, G Major, B minor and the octave of E minor on the 1st string. For the minor triads Rusty uses his 1st, 2nd and 4th fingers, and for the Major triads he uses his 1st, 3rd and 4th fingers.

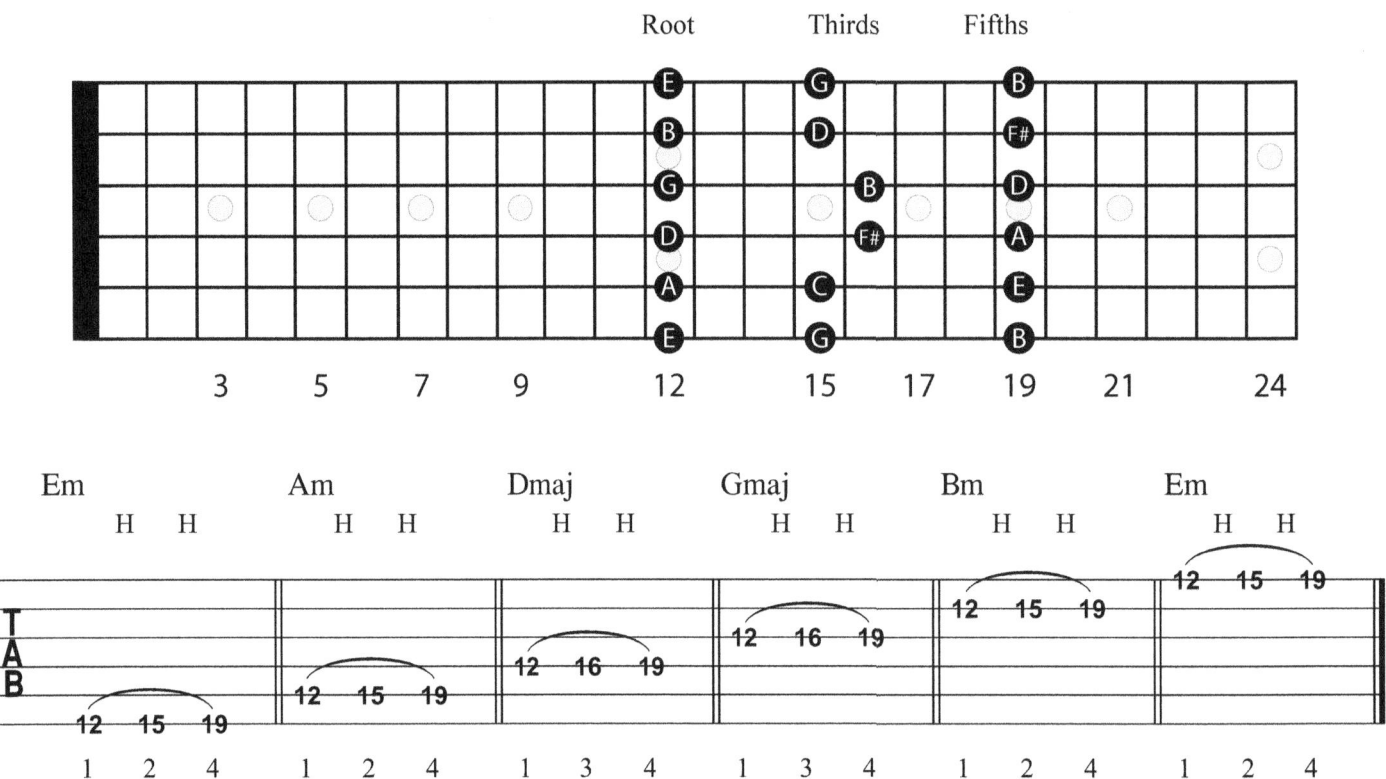

You can play these arpeggios in a variety of ways. Below are two different examples but you should try to experiment and see what else you can come up with.

Traditional ascending & descending with legato

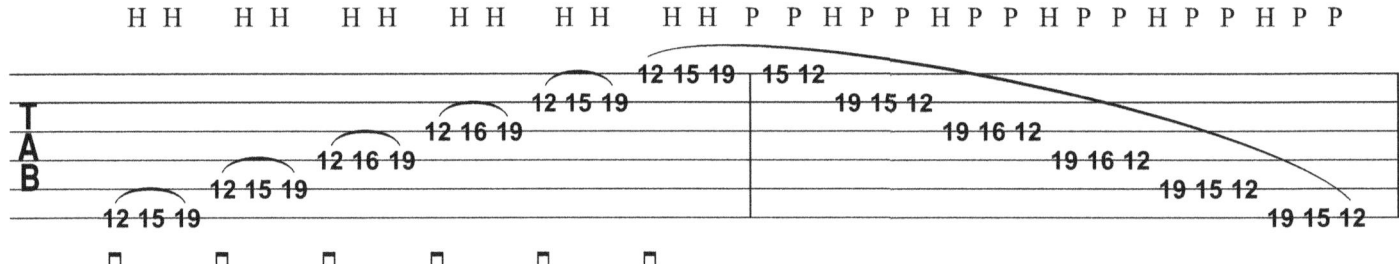

"Ascending - Descending" pattern

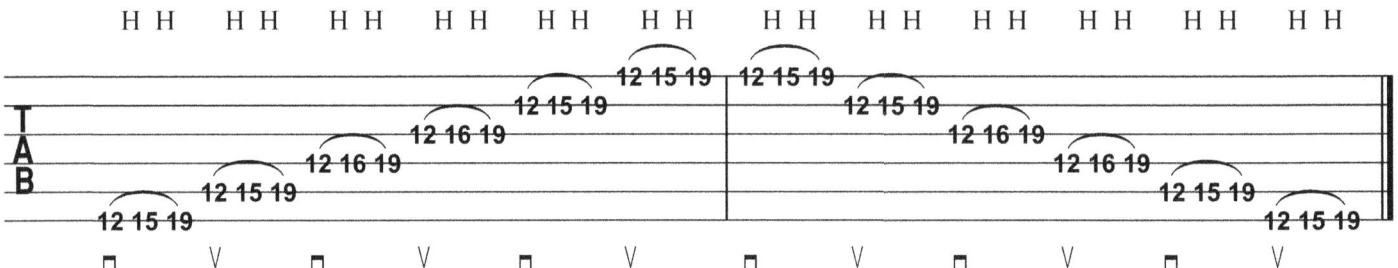

Example 2 Moves up to the 14th position and uses the F# diminished, B minor, E minor, A minor and D Major triads. When we get to the 2nd string we have a half step shift to the 15th fret for the D Major triad, and then back down a half step on the 1st string to the 14th fret for the octave of the F# diminished triad.

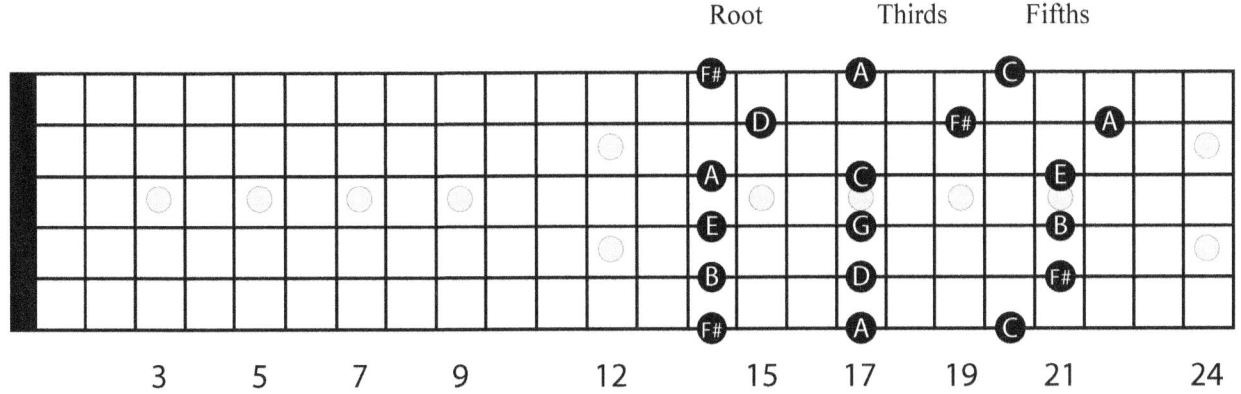

Example 3 uses the 15th through 22nd frets and begins on G Major. This example will play through the triads G Major, C major, E minor, A minor and D Major. The E minor and A minor triads both have a half step shift to the 14th fret.

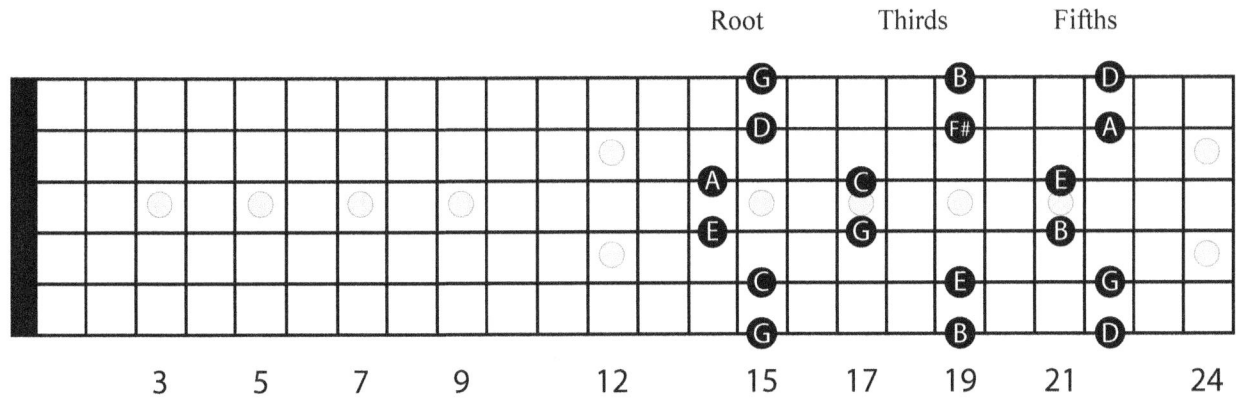

Example 4 uses the 17th through 24th frets and begins on A minor. This example will play through the triads A minor, D Major, G Major, C Major and E minor.

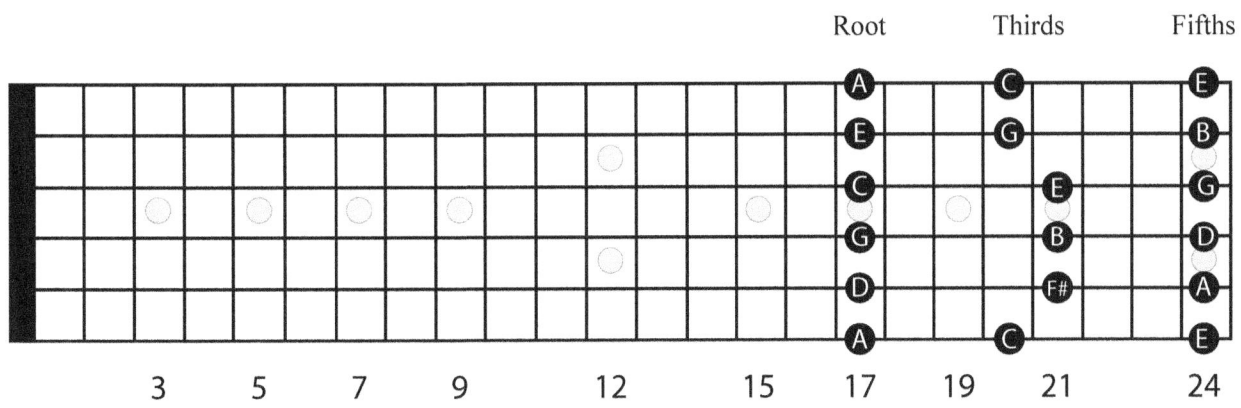

Example 5 shifts down to the 7th position of the neck and plays through the triads: B minor, E minor, A minor, D Major, G Major and C Major. Both the G Major and C Major triads will have a half step shift to the 8th fret on the 1st and 2nd strings.

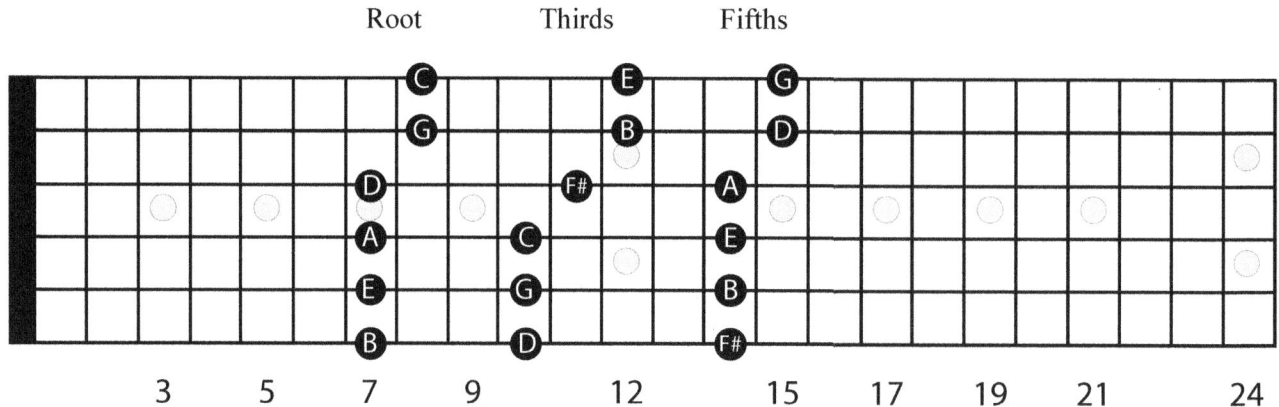

Example 6 begins in the 8th position C note. This position will give us C Major, F# diminished, B minor, E minor, A minor and D Major. Both the A minor and D Major triads will shift a half step to the 10th fret on the 1st and 2nd strings. The F# diminished, B minor and E minor triads will have a half step shift to the 9th fret.

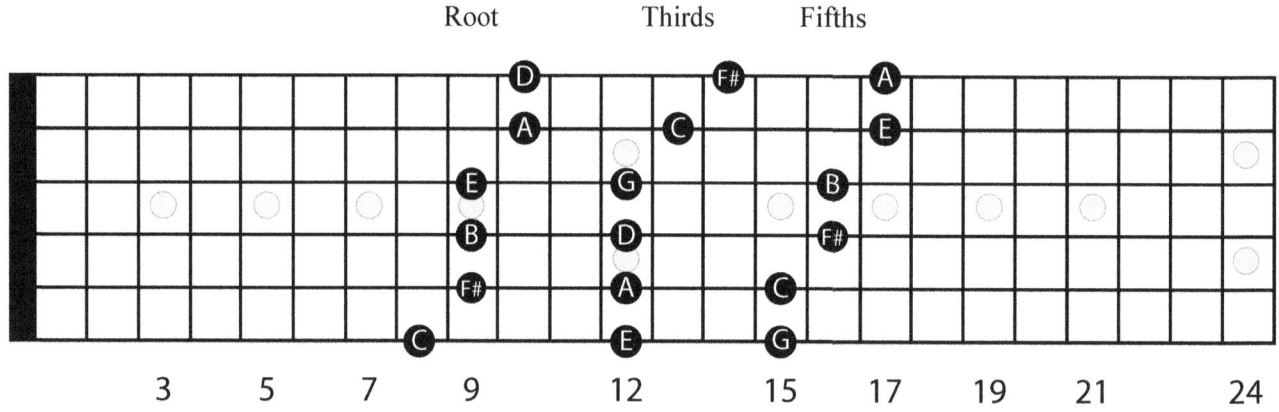

Example 7 begins in the 10th position on D. The triads in this position are D Major, G Major, C Major, F# diminished at the 11th fret, B minor and E minor at the 12th fret.

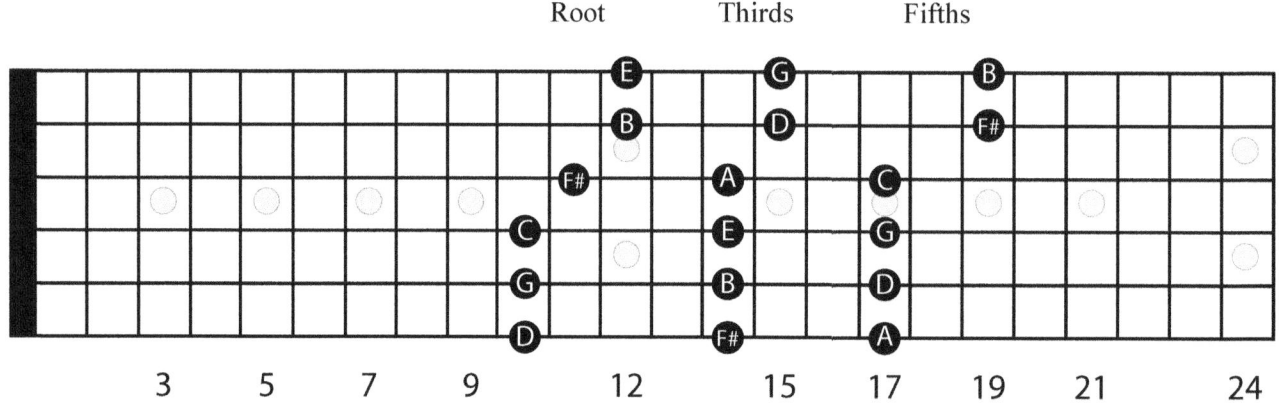

All of these different patterns will work, and work well over any of the seven diatonic chords in the key of "E" minor. Be sure to practice these over all the seven different chords so that you can really get the sound of the harmony these arpeggios create when played in a musical context.

Chapter 23: Song Excerpts from Rusty

The following tabs are all excerpts from Rusty's songs that will be using the different techniques that you learned throughout the programs. Download the free videos that correspond to these songs for free from the *Lesson Support site*.

"Diminium"

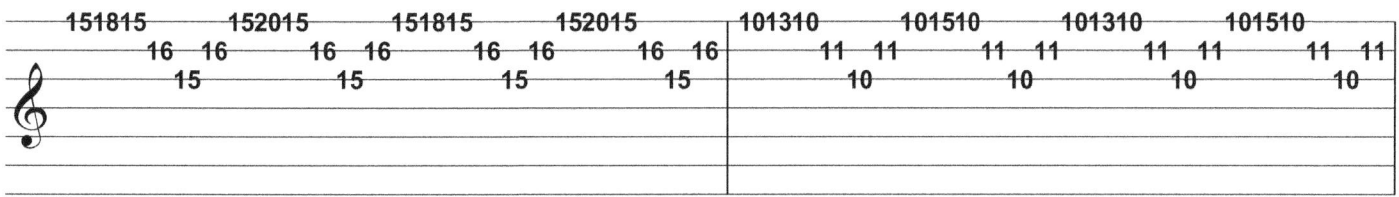

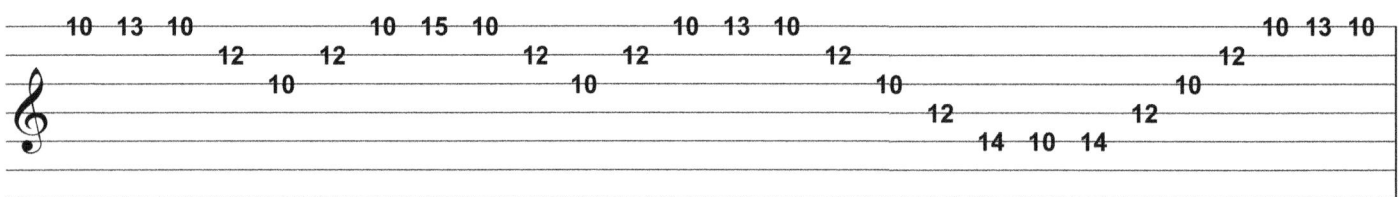

"Riders"

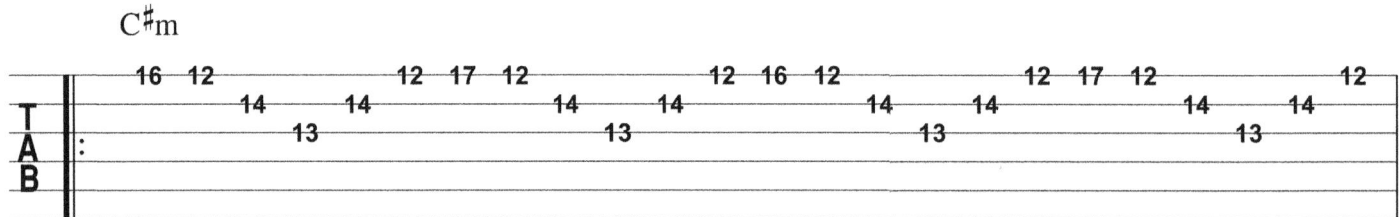

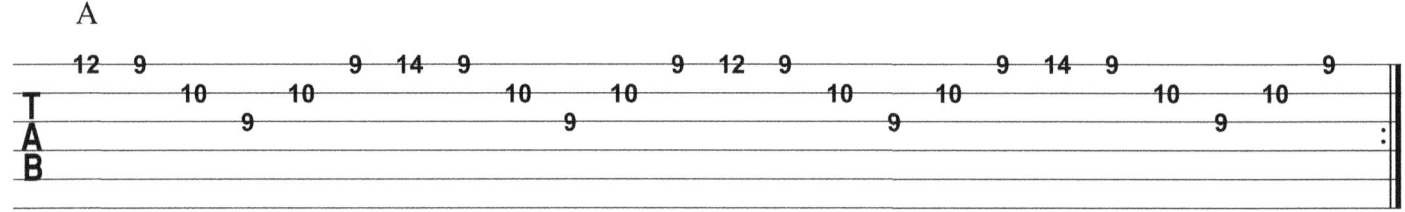

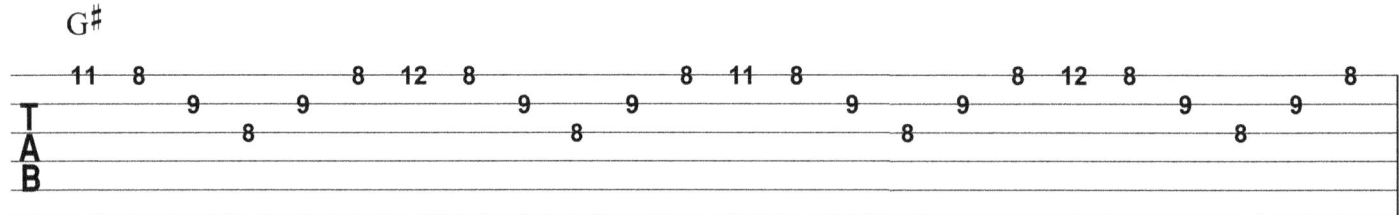

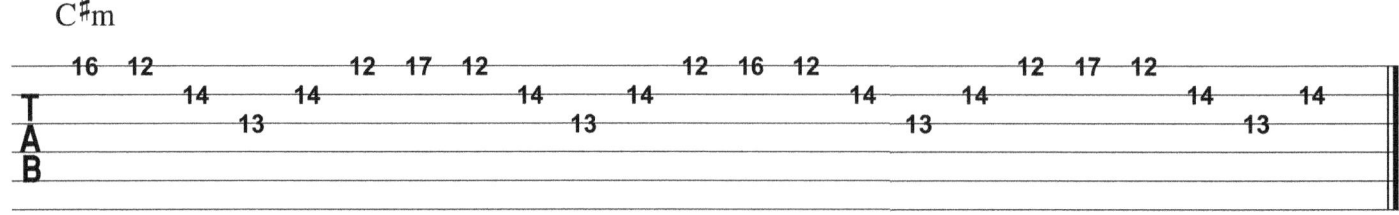

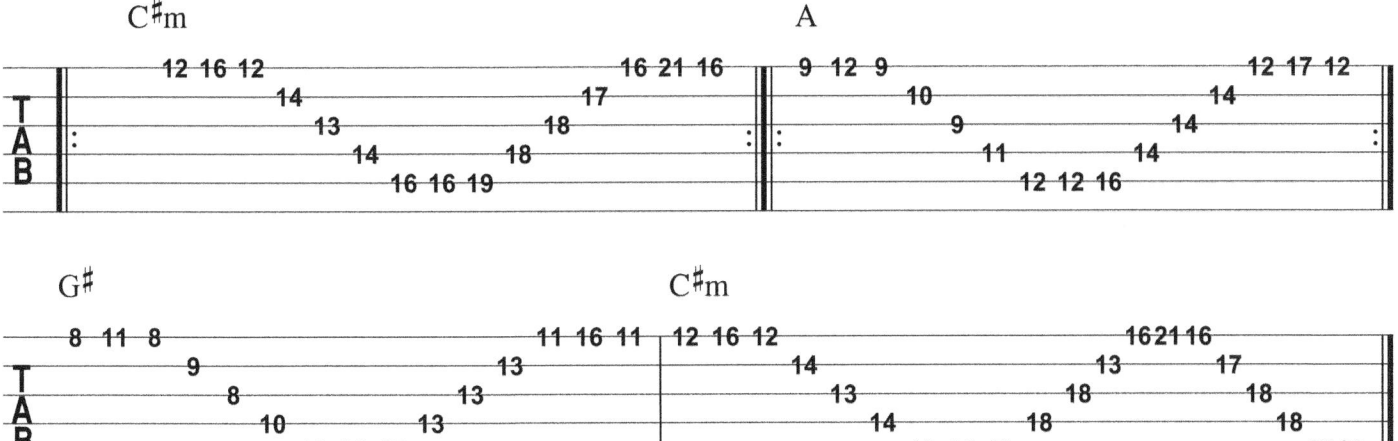

"Riders"
Chorus Arpeggios & Outro Solo

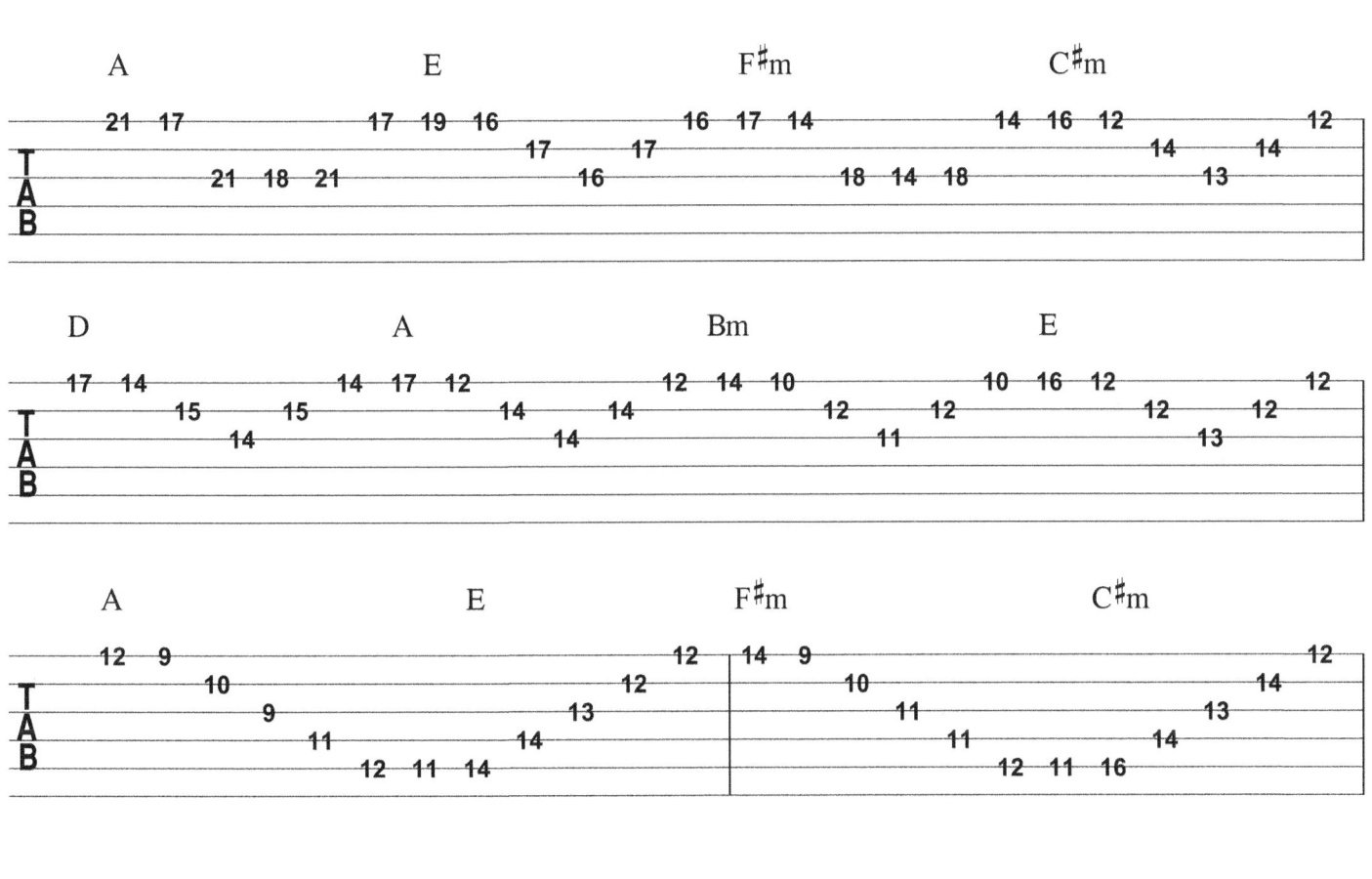

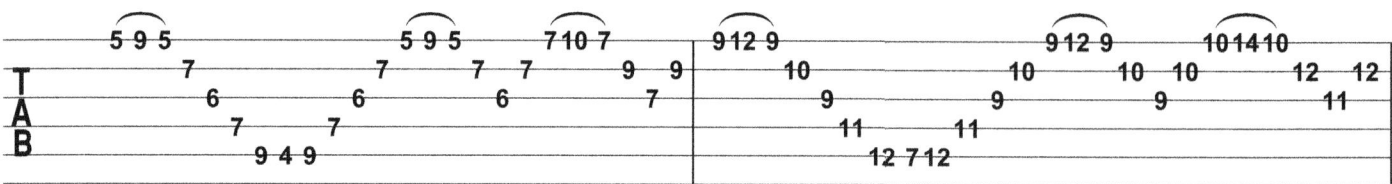

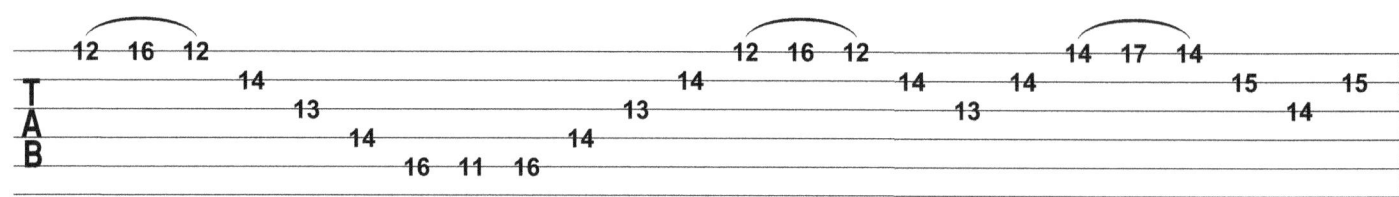

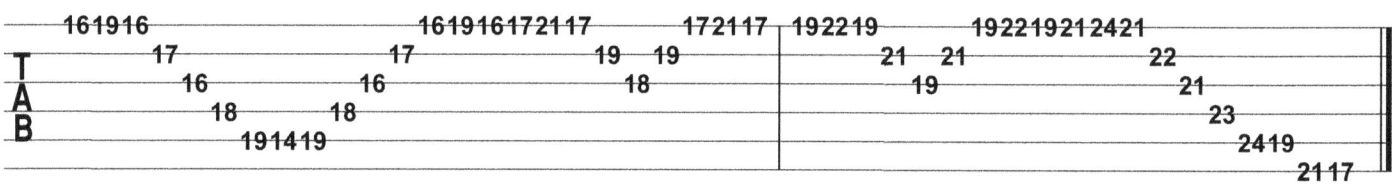

"The Butcher"
Intro

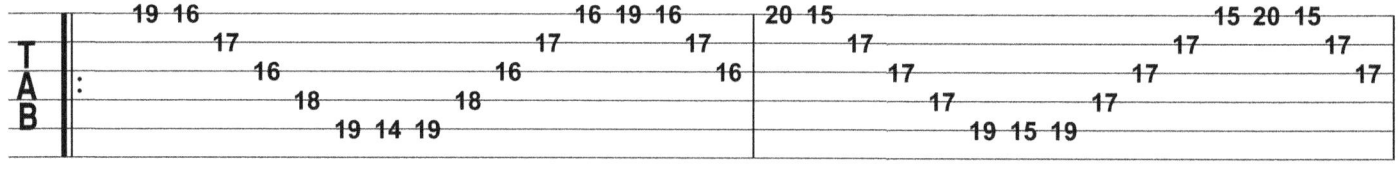

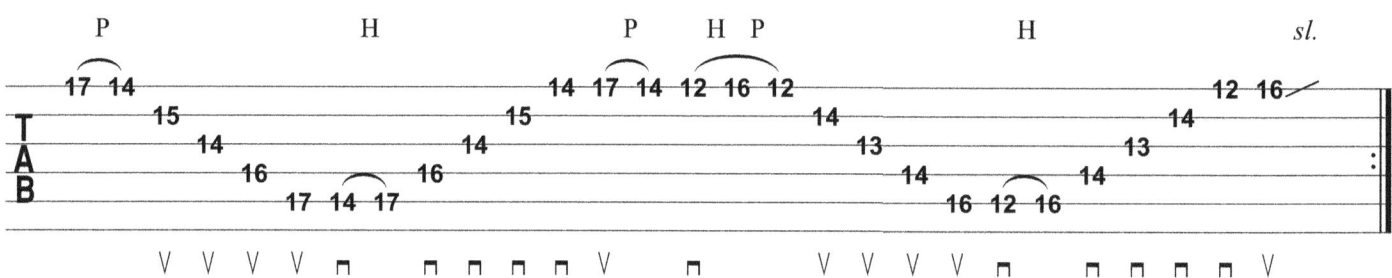

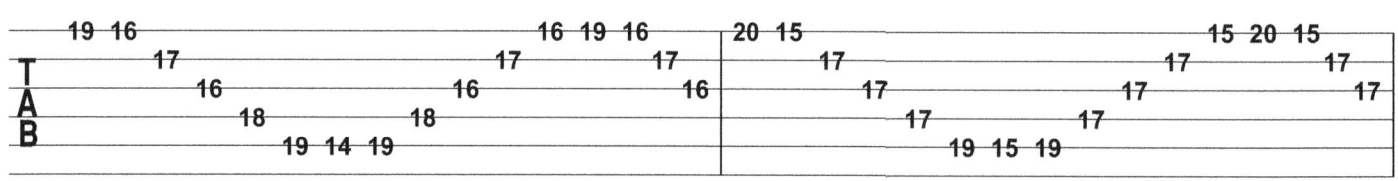

"The Butcher"
Pre Solo

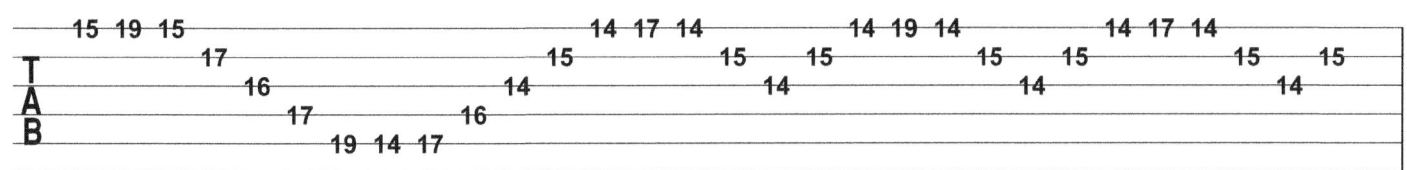
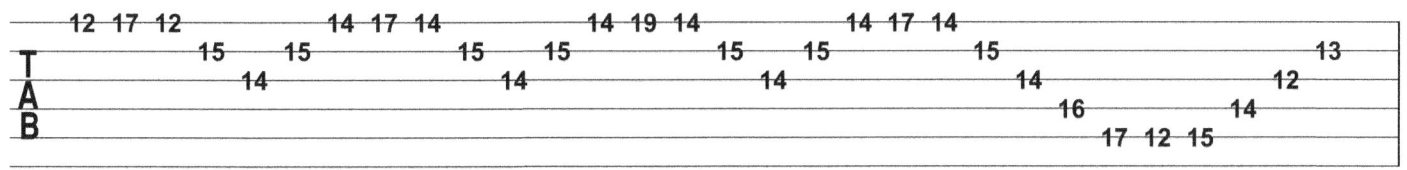

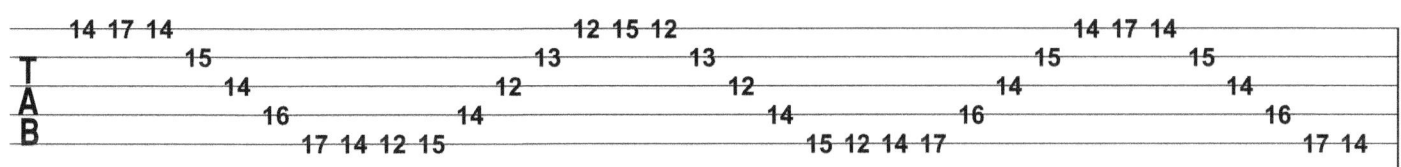
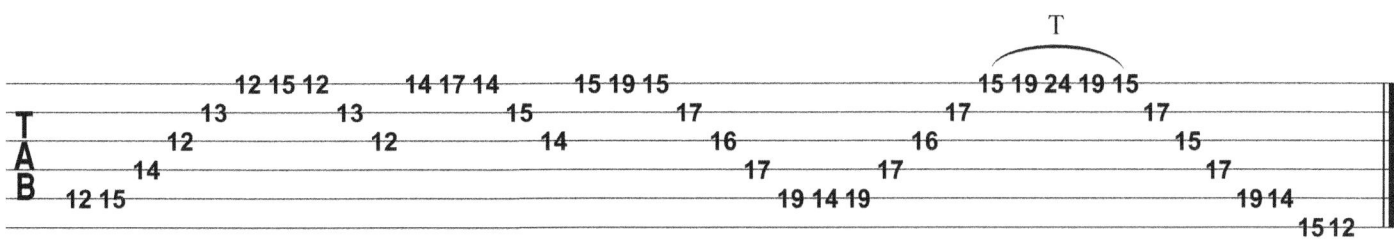

"War Cry"

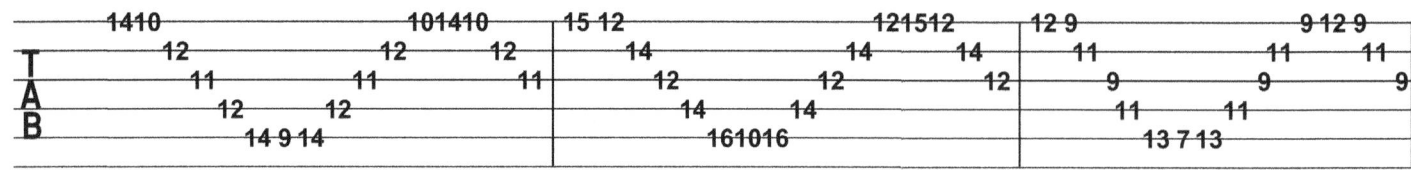

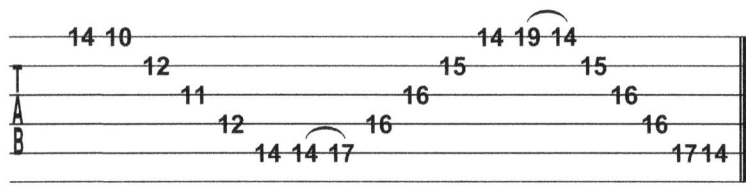

Chord Table

On the next page you you will find a printable chord table chart. You can fill in your scale tones to give you a chart for all of your diatonic chords and arpeggios. Below is an example of the chart filled out with the C Major scale so you can see how the chart works.

	I	**ii**	**iii**	**IV**	**V**	**vi**	**vii**
Degree	1	2/9	3	4/11	5	6/13	7
Root	C	D	E	F	G	A	B
3rd	E	F	G	A	B	C	D
5th	G	A	B	C	D	E	F
7th	B	C	D	E	F	G	A
9th	D	E	F	G	A	B	C
11th	F	G	A	B	C	D	E
13th	A	B	C	D	E	F	G

Triad = Root, 3rd, 5th

Rock House

Degree	I	ii	iii	IV	V	vi	vii
Root	1	2/9	3	4/11	5	6/13	7
3rd							
5th							
7th							
9th							
11th							
13th							

Triad